KNOD/001/005

\

LORD MELBOURNE'S

Susan

by

DOROTHY HOWELL-THOMAS

GRESHAM BOOKS

First published 1978

ISBN 0 905418 25 5

Gresham Books
Unwin Brothers Limited
The Gresham Press
Old Woking
Surrey
England

Typeset by Reproprint, Leatherhead, Surrey.
Printed by Unwin Brothers Ltd., The Gresham Press,
Old Woking, Surrey, England.

FOREWORD

Lord MELBOURNE'S SUSAN is a type of biography we should all welcome, now that so many great figures in history have been thoroughly investigated. It is about an obscure, but interesting character, who throws light on a whole social epoch. Miss Howell-Thomas's study of the mysterious girl in the Melbourne household gives us a new view of the notorious 'Devonshire House set', and in turn, a new appreciation of Regency England. By keen, original research, she disposes of many careless generalisations, and brings us close to the biographer's ideal achievement, the sense of past men and women as they actually were.

It is often said that the biographer is like a detective; certainly this biography's climax is as skilled a piece of documentary detection as one is likely to find. Yet, unlike the detective, the biographer is not out to prove a case. There are no villains or innocents: only fallible human nature. Miss Howell-Thomas judiciously demonstrates this by her convincing conclusion, in which she evokes, in its own terms, the true spirit of a past age.

Robert Gittings

to

Clio, Véronique, and Antoine

and
a belated tribute to

WILLIAM AND CAROLINE LAMB

CONTENTS

FOREWORD   III

PREFACE AND ACKNOWLEDGEMENTS   VII

THE PEOPLE IN THE BACKGROUND
OF THE STORY   XI

INTRODUCTION   1

CHAPTER ONE
Wife, Children and Friends   5

CHAPTER TWO
Brocket Hall   34

CHAPTER THREE
Geneva   64

CHAPTER FOUR
Lausanne   83

CHAPTER FIVE
Marriage   93

EPILOGUE   122

APPENDIX   132

BIBLIOGRAPHY AND SOURCES
OF REFERENCE   138

INDEX   143

V

ILLUSTRATIONS

Poem from book by William Robert Spencer   16

Title Page from *Urania or the Illuminé*
by William Robert Spencer   17

Drawing attributed to Caroline Lamb   36

Account for items for Susan   41

Tradesman's account for drapery items   42

Account rendered by Susan's school mistress   43

Letter from Susan (at Brocket) to
Augustus Lamb   47 & 48

Another letter from Susan to Augustus   49

Drawings of the dogs at Brocket
attributed to Caroline Lamb   53

Drawings by Caroline Lamb   54

Places in Geneva mentioned in Susan's journal   75

Geneva: Saint-Antoine   75

Lord Melbourne's first consent to
Susan's marriage   95

Lord Melbourne's second consent to
Susan's marriage   97

Lord Melbourne's power of attorney to
Susan's Swiss trustees   99 & 100

Views of Vevey showing the Cuénod house   123

Embroidery work by Susan   129

Susan and Aimé Cuénod   129

PREFACE AND ACKNOWLEDGEMENTS

The starting point for this book was a leather-bound volume which lay on my shelves for a number of years before I realised that it contained names which would arouse enough interest to make further research rewarding — the names of Lord Melbourne and Lady Brandon in particular, but others too. The volume is the manuscript journal of a young English girl who had just arrived in Geneva, in 1832, and who began by recording her impressions of the journey from England and then very vividly described her life in Geneva and the people she met there. On the last page was a letter, or memorandum, written much later, in which she told her children about her parentage. Also, tucked into the book, was a copy of a letter which her husband had attached to his will and which was to be read after his death. These documents made it evident that she was the child referred to in various memoirs and biographies as Lord Melbourne's ward, Susan.

From there, apart from family tradition handed down to her Swiss descendants, it was a question of research; and it was an exciting moment when I realised the way in which so many of the documents acknowledged below dovetailed neatly into the events described by Susan, just as the archives in Geneva and Lausanne confirmed, and elucidated, her journal. They also revealed something of Lady Brandon's later history just at the point where she is thought to have disappeared from Lord Melbourne's life.

Far more important, however, was the light which Susan's diary, together with letters in the Panshanger Papers in Hertfordshire Record Office, threw on facets of William and Caroline Lamb's characters and family life. William Lamb, 2nd Viscount Melbourne, has become almost stereotyped as the young Queen Victoria's avuncular Prime Minister, and his wife Lady Caroline as

Byron's clamant lover. Susan's story changes the picture in subtle ways, and increases our respect for them.

Susan wrote her journal swiftly, not as a daily record, but as her thoughts came tumbling out, with no care for paragraphs or punctuation. The extracts that are copied here are reproduced exactly as she wrote. The inconsistencies in her use of accents in French words — sometimes she remembers to put one over an *e* but more often than not it is the wrong accent — have also been left uncorrected. During her school years in Geneva and Lausanne, her French became increasingly idiomatic, and her English deteriorated, as did her English spelling. No attempt has been made in these pages to edit her.

Finally a note on the spelling of Lady Brandon's name. I have deliberately not used the modern Branden, but have kept to her own — and her contemporaries' — use of Brandon, to which her visiting card bears witness.

* * * * *

I HAVE RECEIVED such generous help in my research that it is difficult to record my gratitude. To Mrs A. E. Duncan-Jones I can only say that, without her extensive knowledge of early nineteenth century diaries and letters, and her constant encouragement, I should not have pursued the elusive but fascinating clues which she was always finding. It was she who identified Susan's maternal grandfather as a man known to his contemporaries for his poetry and wit, and, by thus extending the story into the past, added to its interest.

Next, my thanks go to Madame Claude Exchaquet. She introduced me to the State Archives of Geneva and to the Cantonal Archives of Vaud; she also undertook a great deal of detailed research for me in Lausanne. Mr A. P. R. Exchaquet of Geneva filled in some of the gaps which I had left, while Mr Nicolas Exchaquet, of the Periodicals Section of the University Library of Geneva, showed me the rich material which it contains. Mademoiselle Danièle Cuénod was good enough to allow me to use the documents concerning Susan's marriage settlement in the Vaud records.

To Miss Janet Foster, archivist to the British Records Association, I am indebted for tracing, through the Law Society, the present-day successors to the solicitors who dealt with Lord Melbourne's legal business. At this point, one of the two major frustrations which dogged me began: the firm of solicitors who held the correspondence connected with Susan's dowry had destroyed it, fairly recently, along with most of their nineteenth century papers, but had kept an index which proved that it had existed. The correspondence — together with that of other solicitors whose firms are still extant today but who have neither kept their archives nor deposited them in record offices — might have solved the only, but important, mystery which still surrounds Lord Melbourne's ward. The other frustration I share with all those who try to write about the Lambs: the fact that some of Caroline Lamb's papers, for the years 1816 to 1820, in the British Library, are still reserved, and so not available to the public.

I owe grateful thanks to Dr Robert Gittings, who besides generously giving me his time to discuss various aspects of this book, was willing to put at my disposal the experience he had gained in the ways of the Public Record Office when he was working on his book *The Keats Inheritance*. Mr Christopher Baily made it possible for me to consult the Law Society's Library in Brighton. Mr P. M. Wilkinson's knowledge of Byron and of his period was of great help to me.

I wish especially to record my gratitude to the following for permission to quote from or to reproduce documents: the Hertfordshire Record Office and Lady Ravensdale, for the use of the Panshanger Papers, with particular thanks to Mr Peter Walne, County Archivist, and his staff for their patience, and the encouragement they gave me; the Duke of Devonshire and Trustees of the Chatsworth Settlement, and with particular thanks for the kindness of Mr T. Wragg, MBE, TD, Librarian and Keeper of the Devonshire Collections; the Marquis of Lothian for the Lamb Papers at Melbourne Hall, Derbyshire; the Earl of Bessborough to whom I am greatly indebted for the illustration reproduced on page 36; Messrs Longman and the University of Reading Library for the Thomas Moore papers; the Archives d'Etat de Genève; the Archives cantonales vaudoises, and for permission to reproduce the documents on pages 95, 97, 99 and 100; the Archives de la Commune de Lausanne; the British Library: its Department of Printed Books (and for the illustrations on pages 16 and 17), Department of Manuscripts, and Newspaper Library; the Bibliothèque Publique et Universitaire de Genève for the illustrations on page 75.

My thanks are also due to: the Public Record Office; the National Register of Archives; the Derbyshire Record Office and Miss J. C. Sinar, County Archivist; the Essex Record Office and Mr K.C. Newton, County Archivist; the Bodleian Library, Oxford; the Greater London, Middlesex and Surrey Record Offices; the Reference Libraries in Chichester and Brighton; and the Museum and Historical Research Section of the Bank of England and Mr E. M. Kelly, Curator. I owe this introduction to the kindness of Dr G. J. de C. Mead.

Many others whom it is impossible to name here have given me encouragement and help. Needless to say, no one, named or unnamed, bears any responsibility for what I have written.

Dorothy Howell-Thomas
Chichester

X

THE PEOPLE IN THE BACKGROUND OF THE STORY

The Hon. William Robert Spencer
1769 – 1834

poet and wit; member of Devonshire House and other literary and musical circles; cousin in various degrees to most of those listed below

Mrs William Spencer; née Susan Jenison Walworth; first married to Count Spreti
1769 – [1840?]

married William Spencer in 1791

Louisa Georgiana Spencer; later Mrs Edward Canning

William and Susan Spencer's elder daughter

Harriet Caroline Spencer; later Countess von Westerholt
1798 – [1834?]

their younger daughter

George Trevor Spencer (later Bishop of Madras); and Frederick Spencer

their two youngest sons

Count Francis Jenison Walworth

Mrs Spencer's brother

Lady Diana Beauclerk; née Lady Diana Spencer

William Spencer's aunt; Francis Jenison Walworth's mother-in-law; daughter of the 3rd Duke of Marlborough; a well-known amateur artist

Count Charles von Westerholt

German cousin of the William Spencers; Harriet Spencer's husband

Henrietta Ponsonby, Countess of Bessborough; younger daughter of the Earl and Countess Spencer
1761 – 1821

cousin of William Spencer; Susan's godmother

Frederick Ponsonby, 3rd Earl of Bessborough 1758 – 1844	husband of the above; one of Susan's marriage trustees
Lady Caroline Lamb; née Lady Caroline Ponsonby 1785 – 1828	daughter of the Earl and Countess of Bessborough; wife of William Lamb; cousin of Susan through her mother
The Hon. William Spencer Ponsonby; later Lord de Mauley; and his wife Lady Barbara Ponsonby	Caroline Lamb's youngest brother; one of Susan's marriage trustees
William Cavendish, 5th Duke of Devonshire died 1811	Married (1) Lady Georgiana Spencer and (2) Lady Elizabeth Foster
Georgiana Cavendish, Duchess of Devonshire; elder daughter of the Earl and Countess Spencer 1757 – 1806	the centre, with her sister Henrietta Lady Bessborough, of the Whig Devonshire House circle
Lady Harriet Cavendish — 'Hary-o' — later Countess Granville	daughter of the 5th Duke of Devonshire and his wife Georgiana; well-known letter writer; married Lord Granville Leveson Gower who was for many years her aunt Henrietta Bessborough's lover; first cousin of Caroline Lamb
William Spencer Cavendish, Marquis of Hartington, became 6th Duke of Devonshire in 1811 1790 – 1858	only son of 5th Duke of Devonshire and his wife Georgiana; Caroline Lamb's favourite cousin
Lady Elizabeth Foster 1759 – 1824	friend of Georgiana Duchess of Devonshire; mistress of the 5th Duke; married him after the death of his first wife
Caroline St Jules; later Mrs George Lamb	daughter of the 5th Duke of Devonshire and Lady Elizabeth Foster; born before they married, in the life-time of Duchess Georgiana

Elizabeth Lamb, Viscountess Melbourne died 1818	William Lamb's mother; noted hostess of Melbourne House
Emily Countess Cowper; née Emily Lamb	William and George Lamb's sister, who later by her second marriage became Lady Palmerston
The Hon. William Lamb; from 1828 2nd Viscount Melbourne 1779 – 1848	married Lady Caroline Ponsonby in 1805; Queen Victoria's first Prime Minister; Susan's guardian
Augustus Lamb 1807 – 1836	their son; Susan's playfellow
Lady Brandon; née Miss Elizabeth La Touche	Lord Melbourne's mistress
Lilly Crosbie; later Mrs Henry Redhead Yorke	Lord and Lady Brandon's daughter; friend of Susan who called her Rosa
The Hon. Mrs. Norton; née Caroline Sheridan	granddaughter of Richard Brinsley Sheridan and daughter of Tom Sheridan; writer and social pioneer; close friend and confidante of Lord Melbourne
George Spencer (took the name of Spencer-Churchill in 1817); succeeded as 5th Duke of Marlborough in 1817 died 1840	first cousin of William Spencer; owned a famous library which he was obliged to sell; member of Parliament
George Spencer-Churchill, Marquis of Blandford; became 6th Duke of Marlborough in 1840. 1793 – 1857	eldest son of the 5th Duke of Marlborough; member of Parliament for Chippenham; later for Woodstock, Oxon
Miss Susanna Adelaide Law	the Marquis of Blandford's mistress
Sir John Cam Hobhouse; later Lord Broughton	brother-in-law to the Rev. George Trevor Spencer; Lord Byron's friend and executor
Mr John Nelson Darby	one of the founders of the Plymouth Brethren sect.

INTRODUCTION

> At the Duke of Devonshire's Ball were Miss Spencer,
> now Baroness somebody, the Baron, father and mother
> etc. They were the objects of universal curiosity,
> commiseration, contempt, or any other feeling
> according to the good nature of each individual.
>
> *letter from Sydney Smith to Lord Grey*[1]

THE DUKE OF DEVONSHIRE had given the ball early in
1820 at his house in Chiswick for his cousin, formerly Miss Harriet
Spencer. The young Duke was known for his considerate kindness,
especially to any of his relations, and he had invited London
society to the ball in the hope that Harriet might be received once
again after being ostracised for some two years. Her fault had been
in having a child, Susan, before marriage.

Susan's identity was known only to her immediate family and to
those relations, by blood or marriage, who took her into their
homes and brought her up from the time of her birth. In
contemporary letters and diaries she is simply Susan, usually one of
the people in the train of Lady Caroline Lamb. Tradesmen and
school mistresses sent in their bills to be paid for Miss Susan.
Gossip in the Duke of Wellington's circle would have had her the
daughter of Henry de Ros, who was a bachelor. The novelist, Miss
Maria Edgeworth, was told that she was the child of a married
man. Later writers have suggested that her name might have been
St John and that she was the daughter of Melbourne's mistress
Lady Brandon; and this, for reasons that her story will make clear,
is a plausible though incorrect deduction.

Her name was Susan Harriett Elizabeth Churchill.[2] Her
maternal grandfather was the poet and wit, William Robert
Spencer, whose cousin, George Spencer-Churchill, fifth Duke of

1

Marlborough, was, according to information later given to Susan, her paternal grandfather. That the Duke's son George, Marquis of Blandford, and William Spencer's daughter Harriet, did not marry, though both were free to do so, remains part of the mystery which still surrounds the child Susan. Yet much of the cousins' story becomes understandable in the light of the complex personal, social, moral, political and financial relationships of the large family circle of Spencers and Marlboroughs, Bessboroughs, Melbournes and Devonshires. The personalities and behaviour of Harriet Spencer's own parents reveal something of the insecurity of her childhood and youth, which was part of, and to some extent an inheritance from, the later, sadder, less glorious days of that entity and culture which the words Devonshire House convey. Susan herself is on the fringe of that group of children, who have been called 'Children of the Mist',[3] born earlier of the manifold friendships and loves of Devonshire House.

The importance of Susan's story lies in the circumstances of her life, for they reveal hitherto unnoticed aspects of the characters of Lady Bessborough and her husband, the third Earl, and especially do they alter the inherited image which we have of William and Caroline Lamb. The light they throw is a refracted light only, because Susan did not keep a childhood journal nor did she write reminiscences of her life at Brocket, the Lambs' country home — would that she had: her journal begins in Geneva when she was in her fifteenth year. But the very fact that William and Caroline, to whom tradition attributes so tormented a family life, so little consistency, responsibility and generosity, brought her up and set her on her way to adulthood, and watched over her with affection to the end of their lives, speaks as only facts can. Her existence also lightens, just a little, the gloomy sadness which tradition, again, has cast over the last years of Caroline's life.

In a real sense, therefore, even if at one remove, we see these people, with some of their children, their friends, their doctors and their servants, through the eyes of the child Susan. They grow in stature in the process. Lady Bessborough, who had of course known her young cousin Harriet Spencer from childhood, takes the baby Susan at birth and has her looked after in her house at Roehampton. Her daughter Caroline Lamb continues to care for her when Lady Bessborough dies. The presence of the 'mysterious child' at Brocket has been said to have been a 'whim'[4] of Lady Caroline's; on the contrary, Caroline was, it seems, accepting a trust inherited from her mother which continued until her own death. Then Lord Melbourne, though with less enthusiasm, sees to Susan's education until her marriage, and even beyond that continues to act as one of the trustees of her marriage settlement.

Two other women, Lady Brandon and Mrs Norton, respectively mistress and — it must be believed on his solemn word, no more than — close friend of Melbourne, touched Susan's life in some degree, as did, in care and kindness to her, Lord Bessborough and his sons after their sister Caroline's death.

Susan's life reflects the transition from Regency to Victorian England — Regency that is in atmosphere if not strictly in date. Lady Bessborough was in reality, and William and Caroline Lamb were in essence, and certainly intellectually, of the eighteenth century. When John Murray the publisher was asked why Byron never wrote anything that women might properly read, that was the nineteenth century speaking; but when Caroline Lamb, with her independent, educated and questioning mind, read 'Don Juan', she said, 'I cannot tell you how clever I think it is, in my heart'.[5] This was the eighteenth century's objective appreciation of literary skill with no thought for its propriety or its suitability for one sex or the other.

Caroline's farcical masquerades and exhibitionist outings at Brocket were no more than an exaggerated form of that free, unselfconscious though often arrogant behaviour which marked contemporary English aristocracy. The tomboyishness, as well as the courage in riding and climbing, just as much as the polished manners, and ability to write well in English or French which Susan showed as a girl in Geneva, these were her inheritance from a boisterous as well as a civilised, intelligent childhood at Brocket. She was a child of her age in other ways too: as she grew out of her girlhood, she was easily moved to romantic passion, and with that went a curious innocence, very like the youthful Caroline's, that 'wild innocence, the barbaric purity, of the creature who had been brought up, an uncontaminated savage, in the splendour and corruption of Devonshire House'.[6] Susan displayed none of that coyness with men which marked girls in the later part of the century. Later, after her marriage in the year of Queen Victoria's accession, she changed and, under the influence of the founder of the Plymouth Brethren sect, adopted a biblical evangelical style which would have shocked Lord Melbourne. But her independence of mind and her humorous, critical appraisal of motives and actions did not desert her. Her childhood in the Lambs' household may well have prevented her from becoming a prim, self-effacing wife, and perhaps have prepared her to be, as in a sense she eventually was, her husband's business partner.

If ease of writing, with genuine feeling and a light-hearted self-mockery, can be inherited, then Susan owed that gift to her grandfather, William Robert Spencer. Apart from short dictionary notices, his biography has not been written since his devoted admirer, Miss Louisa Poulter, composed a memoir of him immediately after his death. As it was his connections which created an adoptive family for Susan and saved her from the destitution and social contempt suffered by so many children born outside marriage, it is fitting to begin the story of Lord Melbourne's ward with an account of her maternal grandfather.

NOTES

1. *Letters of Sydney Smith,* edited by Nowell C. Smith; letter from Sydney Smith to Lord Grey, April 1820.
2. *Journal.* This abbreviation will be used throughout as a general reference to Susan's diary.
3. *Miss Eden's Letters,* edited by Violet Dickinson.
4. *The Letters of Caroline Norton to Lord Melbourne,* (editors) James O. Hoge and Clarke Olney; footnote on page 31.
5. Quoted by Elizabeth Jenkins in her *Lady Caroline Lamb.*
6. Elizabeth Jenkins, op. cit.

CHAPTER ONE

Wife, Children and Friends

The day-spring of youth, still unclouded with sorrow,
 Alone on itself for enjoyment depends,
But drear is the twilight of age if it borrow
 No warmth from the smiles of *wife, children,* and *friends.*

*from the ballad 'Wife, Children and Friends',
by W. R. Spencer*

THE MODERN BIOGRAPHER of William Robert Spencer is faced with paradox and irony. Here was a man whose family connections and whose personal gifts promised the brightest future, who yet died a penurious exile. His poetry spoke of the love of wife and children: his marriage foundered, he was accused of neglecting his children's moral upbringing, and for one of his daughters this led to tragedy. A man in public so irresistibly amusing that for years his anecdotes and mimicry were remembered, was with his own family morose and silent. He was clever, an excellent linguist, and a sensitive user of his own language; but all that he is now remembered by is a collection of light society verse and an opera or two; while some of his serious and 'moving poetry does not deserve to have been so well forgotten. He had, without doubt, an innate charm and friendliness, but he was weak, and, with an unhappy marriage and heavy debts, became increasingly addicted to brandy and laudanum. He had the intelligence and articulateness, as well as the rank, to have made his mark in politics; yet as the years went by he was despised and written of with contempt — 'never solid, never steady'.[1]

It is ironic that his sole contemporary biographer, Miss Louisa Poulter, was a woman who knew him only in the last four years of his life, when he was an exile in Paris. She venerated him as a disciple would her master; but most of what she wrote of him was told to her by him. She was however unlikely to have been quite as naive as Walter Scott's biographer Lockhart would have us believe: '. . . her chef d'oeuvre — the solemn canonization of the pure and holy [William Robert Spencer] whose delirium tremens of brandy she took for edifying proof of religious ecstasy'.[2]

Nonetheless it was of William Spencer that Walter Scott thought as he meditated on the unfulfilled promise of many a dying life: 'Those fine lines of Spencer come into my head —

> The shade of youthful hope is there,
>   That lingered long and latest died;
> Ambition all dissolved to air,
>   With phantom honours by his side.
> What empty shadows glimmer nigh?
>   They once were Friendship, Truth, and Love! . . .

Ay, and can I forget the author — the frightful moral of his own vision?'[3]

By kinship and by inclination, William Spencer belonged to the Devonshire House circle. Devonshire House — which describes a way of life, of thought, speech and feeling — owed its genius to the people at the centre of that characteristic group of Whigs who met in the Duke's house in Piccadilly or in any of the country houses where they might be staying.

Its greatness spanned the married life of Georgiana, Duchess of Devonshire, who married the Duke when barely seventeen, in 1774, and died in 1806. Georgiana and her sister Henrietta were the daughters of the Earl and Countess Spencer. Their mother was an upright, devout, serious woman, who in her widowhood lived the life of an English country gentlewoman, with a regular daily time-table, a concern for the education of the poor, and an interest in her garden. In her youth she had often travelled on the Continent, and as a married woman had known foreign courts, particularly that of Louis XVI and Marie-Antoinette, who was a friend and always took a genuine interest in Lady Spencer's daughters. All this had given her a degree of sophistication, but she lacked the sparkling charm of her daughters. Georgiana and

6

Henrietta throughout their lives kept their sense of family devotion and the simple piety they had learned from their mother; but their marriages into the glittering setting in which the fashionable Whig world spent itself led them both into a morass of debt which remained a constant source of worry to Lady Spencer. She herself, as she admitted, was not without guilt and had sometimes been carried away by the gambling fever; but her blunt letters about their 'idle dissipation'⁴ never prevented her from helping them financially in so far as she was able.

There had been no Duchess of Devonshire for twenty years when Georgiana Spencer became Georgiana Cavendish, wife of the fifth Duke of Devonshire. A few years afterwards, Henrietta married Frederick Ponsonby, later to be the third Earl of Bessborough. The charm and intelligence of the two sisters were the initial attraction to Devonshire House. The Duchess had a kindness and a capacity for faithful friendship, to both men and women, which illuminated the beauty for which she was famous. Henrietta Bessborough was cleverer, but as loving and as romantic as her sister. Both had been educated into that true eighteenth century erudition, so soundly based in the classics and in French, with no tinge of the blue-stocking, but only a peculiar grace of its own.

The friendship between the Whig statesman, Charles James Fox, and the Duchess soon made Devonshire House a lively political centre. Fox was its idol, welcomed, campaigned for, and loved by everyone — deservedly so, for he too had, above all his brilliance and renowned charm, a genius for enduring friendship. The sense of exhilaration of those years, compounded of enthusiastic political activity, brilliant conversation, theatrical amusements — Sheridan, playwright and politician, belonged to the circle — travelling abroad or to the great country houses, was overshadowed by the contemporary addiction to gambling. Led by Fox, who had early ruined himself at the tables, in Paris and in London, Georgiana and Henrietta threw themselves into gaming, and were forever after tormented by the knowledge of debts which they had not the means to pay. The list of their creditors was without end, and the complicated tissue of loans, repayments at interest, and further loans became the fixed pattern of their lives and the frightening background of every relationship and every pleasure.

But it is their close family links, their letters to each other, their agonising over and loving of their children, legitimate and illegitimate, for which these people are best remembered. The genuinely warm, loving nature of the Duchess, and perhaps even more of Lady Bessborough, redeemed whatever was shallow in Devonshire House. Family ties were also strong among their children. The Devonshires had two daughters, of whom Lady Harriet Cavendish — Hary-o — is the often-quoted letter-writer; and a son, the Marquis of Hartington. The Bessboroughs had three sons, and a daughter, Lady Caroline Ponsonby, five years older than her beloved cousin Hartington, her 'dear Hart'.

William Spencer's older children were near contemporaries of these, and his fourth child, Harriet, born in 1798, was thirteen years younger than Caroline Ponsonby. These younger ones also spent some of their time with the group of children. 'Little Harrio Spencer', wrote Lady Bessborough to her lover Lord Granville Leveson Gower, 'cries after you, and wants a horse to ride after you and fetch you back. But, oh disgrazia! She took Lord Ossulston for you this eve^g at dessert'.[5] Harriet had not realised that Lord Granville was tall and of a god-like beauty, whereas Lord Ossulston was so small that he was called 'little o'. The older girls at Devonshire House had grown up with a daughter of a French émigré, the Duc de Grammont, and there was much romantic talk among them when she and 'little o' became engaged.

The tribe of Devonshire House children were a group of cousins most of whom grew up in its own peculiar culture, its ethos. They were stamped with its mannerisms (though they made fun of its drawling speech), and its rejection of conventions together with its concern for outward propriety. They shared its learning, its art, its fun and its ardent Whiggery. Their internal likes and dislikes — Caroline Ponsonby was always much fonder of her Cavendish girl cousins than they were of her — were not apparent outside the eminently aristocratic, cultured circle. Almost all of them left their mark on the political or literary history of England.

Some years later, two ladies were discussing that earlier, brilliant Devonshire House society. 'Does it strike you', asked one of the other, 'that vices are wonderfully prolific among the Whigs? There are such countless illegitimates among them, such a tribe of Children of the Mist . . .'.[6]

This is another curiously baffling aspect of the characters of people who in general were affectionate marriage partners, certainly loving parents, and in many cases sincerely religious. There were factors common to all these children which Harriet

Spencer's daughter Susan Churchill — of the next generation — did not share. They were born of married women; their mothers discreetly disappeared during pregnancy and the children were born abroad; they were cherished and cared for by their parents, living either in their mother's home or with relations or with wholly trustworthy retainers; they did not bear their father's name though often they were given that of some property belonging to him. They frequently lived — and this was by no means unusual in the eighteenth century — with their legitimate half brothers and sisters. Not until the time came for their marriages was there any social concern about them. But the important difference between these 'children of the mist' and Susan was that their birth was supposed to be a matter of knowledge only within the limited family circle — the Duchess of Devonshire was afraid of her mother learning the parentage (the Duke of Devonshire and Lady Elizabeth Foster) of the pretty child Caroline St Jules due to come from France to Devonshire House — whereas Harriet Spencer's seduction was public knowledge.

There was indeed a tribe of them. Charles Grey — later the Lord Grey of the Reform Bill — and Georgiana Devonshire had a daughter of whom outside gossips learnt only because of the Duchess' frequent visits to Lord Grey's parents who were bringing her up. The long and faithful love affair between Henrietta Bessborough and Lord Granville Leveson Gower produced two children. Caroline St Jules was the daughter of the Duke of Devonshire and Lady Elizabeth Foster. Lady Elizabeth had first come to Devonshire House when, after an unhappy marriage and with two children to educate, she had been befriended by the warm-hearted Duchess, and was put in charge of the education of yet another child of the mist, Charlotte Williams, the result of an earlier liaison between the Duke and a clergyman's daughter, a Miss Spencer. Lady Elizabeth's friendship for the Duchess, which was warmly returned, endured through all the years of this curious triangular relationship, itself ending only with Georgiana's death.

Susan Churchill, born long after, child of the younger generation, was a child of the mist in that she is surrounded by mystery, but she is not typical. Many of the people in that circle, however, were greatly to affect her own life. The scandal caused by her birth was the result of her mother's unmarried state as well as of her unfortunate reputation. It was part of the well-understood ethos of Devonshire House that only married women might indulge in such liaisons. Affairs of the heart must not be the cause of open scandal but must be treated with discretion. If Caroline Lamb had not so blatantly proclaimed and exhibited her love for Byron, she would have escaped, as her mother Lady Bessborough did earlier, the scathing social condemnation which she suffered. Scandal was to be avoided; discreet unfaithfulness within marriage was acceptable.

The earlier arbiter of this social code had been Lady Melbourne, William Lamb's mother. A woman of acute intelligence, with which went beauty, money, and a subtle attraction for men, she had known how to use her lovers to forward her social purposes, of which the overwhelming one was the advancement of her family and in particular of her son William. She had managed to have her children all safely under her husband's name, and there is no proof that they were not his. But Lord Egremont was supposed to be the father of William Lamb; and to the Prince of Wales, later Prince Regent and then George IV, was attributed the paternity of her youngest son George Lamb.

Lady Melbourne's character, calculating but outwardly charming — Byron, though of a younger generation, thought her one of the most attractive women he had ever met, and greatly valued her friendship — contrasted sharply with Lady Bessborough's loving though sometimes weak and foolish nature. Well might Lady Bessborough's own remark about Charles Fox have been made about herself: '. . . kindness and weakness itself to everything that [she] loves . . . '.[7] And yet she too had that discretion which kept her children by Lord Granville in the background. She had the elegant, aristocratic code of her times; and Lady Melbourne's sense of outrage at the public scandal which her daughter-in-law Caroline Lamb created over her affair with Lord Byron was all the more bitter because her ambition had welcomed the marriage of William Lamb into that enchanted Devonshire House circle where, as a young bachelor, he had been an *habitué*.

*   *   *   *   *

AT THE AGE of twenty, William Spencer, talented, witty, at home in this clever, happy, yet oddly amoral society, already sharing the bane of money troubles with his contemporaries, faced a life that was gradually to separate this undoubtedly engaging young man from all these cousins and friends and was to end in loneliness and sadness.

Spencer had been unusually fortunate in his education. He had loved Harrow and was stimulated to work there. Then before going to Oxford, where he did not take a degree, he spent six months under the tutorship of Dr Parr. This celebrated teacher used to take a few students into his vicarage for private tuition, where they had the run of his magnificent library. His method of teaching, one of discussion and conversation, with which today we are familiar, was well suited to Spencer's mind. Dr Parr was a fine Latinist; later, even his critical friends realised that Spencer was a good classical scholar. Like a number of literary men of his time, he owed a good deal to this master.

William Spencer's family life during his childhood had not been equally happy. His father, Lord Charles Spencer, a younger son of the third Duke of Marlborough, and his mother were, by the time he was fifteen, on the brink of a separation. 'I have this instant seen a most wretched being, Ld Charles Spencer', Georgiana Duchess of Devonshire wrote to her mother, '. . . on his coming to town his family and relations have shewn him that on his son's [there was also an elder son, John Spencer] acc^t he must be parted; he will not hear of a divorce. I believe he is going to Chiswick with Wm Spencer, but do write him a kind line.'[8]

The Grand Tour, when the time came, was thorough, and took Spencer to Germany and to many of that country's courts; to Switzerland and Italy; and to France. He became outstandingly fluent, even in that age of linguists, in Italian, German and French, though later his translations from Italian were criticised as having a number of errors.

Young Englishmen were made welcome at the French Court, and still attended even after the Revolution of 1789 had begun its rumblings. A little known characteristic of Louis XVI was his knowledge of English and his interest in contemporary English literature. Therefore a presentable young English poet, who also had a witty turn of phrase, son of an aristocratic family, would be doubly welcome, especially as so many of his relations were on terms of friendship with the King and Queen. So close did William Spencer get to the French royal family, that he was in the room at Versailles where Louis and Marie-Antoinette and the former Director General of Finances Necker were waiting for the Paris mob, at that moment approaching after marching from Paris. It was the evening of 5 October 1789, and Necker with his obstinate policies bore a heavy responsibility for the events of that year. William Spencer 'heard the Queen of France herself say to M. Necker, "What are we going to do? Speak, say a word, it depends on you." Necker sat in a corner, he was *bien poudré*, and held a great pocket handkerchief to his eyes. He spoke not a word.'[9] Years later, Spencer told this story to Necker's daughter, Madame de Staël, by then as famous a writer as an opponent of Napoleon. She, who had worshipped her father, not unnaturally found it unbearably painful and violently told Spencer never to mention it to her again.

William Spencer had a link with a number of the German courts through his aunt, Lady Diana Beauclerk. Lady Di, as she was known, had a daughter married to Count Francis Jenison Walworth. This German title, prefixing an English name, was the result of an interesting family migration. A Jenison of Walworth in County Durham had emigrated to Germany towards the last quarter of the eighteenth century. There his son Francis had risen fast, first at the court of the Elector Palatine of Bavaria, and then as minister to the Margrave of Hesse-Darmstadt, who sent him as envoy to the Court of St James. Finally he was appointed high chamberlain to the Prince of Würtemberg, whom Napoleon was to make King in 1805. Francis Jenison Walworth had a sister, Susan, who in 1791 was already the widow of Count Spreti, formerly chamberlain to the Margrave of Hesse-Darmstadt.

In their snobbish way, the English among themselves treated this Anglo-German ennobled family as *parvenus*. There is, it must be said, a certain shadiness about them: a hint, for instance, that Count Francis was made minister to the Margrave because he was the favourite of the Margravine. The Jenison Walworths were constantly begging Lady Diana to find them a position in England. 'It is impossible for me to find out', she wrote to her son-in-law, 'how far the great person [the Prince of Wales, later George IV?] dislikes you, or whether he really does dislike you — I have employed different people, but there is no getting at the truth . . . the only bad thing in being refused here would be the possibility of its hurting you in other courts . . .'.[10] One might have expected an official of the Court of Würtemberg, whose Prince remained throughout the war an ally of Napoleon, in spite of his marriage to the Princess Royal of England, to have been *persona non grata* in any event. But journals and letters of the time are curiously free from national animosities. The Princess of Würtemberg wrote to England trying to persuade her mother, the Queen, that 'Buonaparte is much belied!!'[11]

Then there was the Countess Spreti, born Susan Jenison Walworth. Here again there were unpleasant rumours. Count Spreti, it was said, had committed suicide so that his wife might be free to marry Spencer. On the other hand, rumours of violent death were easily raised at the Court of Würtemberg: the Prince himself had imputed to him the murder of his first wife; he then married the Princess Charlotte Augusta, daughter of George III. It was also said that he beat her. But she, having, like her sisters, for years begged her eldest brother, the Prince of Wales, to find her a husband, was in no position to complain of what matrimony, once achieved, might bring.

The marriage, in 1791, of William Spencer to Susan Spreti was represented, by gossips in England, 'as a gross take-in concerted by the brother and the Margravine'. They might have added 'and the mother', for the Dowager Countess Jenison Walworth, Susan Spreti's mother, was maid of honour to the Margravine. It seems that William Spencer's name was worth more in the eyes of the Jenisons than a good annual income, when the Countess Spreti became 'Mrs William Spencer who instead of having a jointure of £10,000 a year which she forfeited on marrying him . . . had only . . . about £40 a year as the widow of an old Chamberlain of the Margrave'.[12]

The auspices appeared unfavourable to the marriage, and in spite of William Spencer's later declaration that he was 'indebted to Germany for all the blessings of domestic happiness!',[13] nothing in the coming years ever indicated that those auspices had been wrong.

*　　*　　*　　*　　*

WHEN MR AND MRS William Spencer returned to England after their marriage they rented a house in London at 36, Curzon Street. Mrs Spencer never became one of the great Whig hostesses; but her drawing-room gathered much of the political and literary society of the time. Fox; Sheridan; Sydney Smith the delightful and witty clergyman; Samuel Rogers and Thomas Moore among the

13

poets; all met at the Spencers. At one time, William made himself acceptable to the Prince of Wales when he was somewhat mysteriously 'employed in governing the P. of W: Lady J[ersey?] all in love with him!!!'[14]

One of the places remembered by Charles Fox and his Whig friends as well as by William Spencer with pleasure and affection was Woolbeding, in Sussex. William's uncle, Lord Robert Spencer, had bought the property, in the Rother Valley, near Midhurst, with a fortune gained from keeping the gaming bank at Brooks's club. He altered and rebuilt the small country house and furnished it in contemporary style. Here Charles Fox often came, and read, and talked, and listened sympathetically to Lady Diana Beauclerk's presentation of petitions on behalf of her son-in-law Count Francis Jenison Walworth. And on everyone Fox as always laid the spell of his immense charm. 'He lived the friend of Fox' was to be Lord Robert Spencer's epitaph.[15] Lady Di, who had been Diana Spencer, daughter of the third Duke of Marlborough (William's grandfather), had had her share of notoriety when, two days after her divorce from her husband, she married Topham Beauclerk, Dr Johnson's friend. She was a fashionable and indeed a gifted amateur artist in her own right. She had illustrated Dryden's *Fables*, and had designed for Wedgwood. For Horace Walpole she painted some murals at Strawberry Hill, and she worked with her nephew William Spencer to illustrate his first major poem, 'Leonore'. The action-filled but gloomy pictures which his English version of the German ballad called for are strangely unlike her art. She sketched Fox, but his clever, dark face was not suited to her style either: the fashionable, romantic, light drawing of cherubs, and pretty women in flowing draperies, flowers and garlands: small, delicate ephemera.

Spencer was becoming well known as a writer of society verse and of translations and imitations of the romantic 'Gothick' ballads about ghostly night-riders and dying maidens that were much in vogue. His opera *Urania or the Illuminé*, which was played at the Theatre Royal, Drury Lane and for which his brother John Spencer composed the music, was openly a burlesque of German tales of doomed lovers. He hoped not to give offence by this reference to one of the few 'slight shades of error' in the German character. His translation of Gottfried Bürger's 'Leonore', a ballad of spectres and open graves and phantom horses, soon became one of his best known works. The subject fascinated other poets too:

Walter Scott's imitation of the German ballad was among his earliest poetry.

William's feeling for shades of language and his sensitiveness to forms of expression different from his own are most clearly shewn in his ballad 'Bethgelert'. 'Gelert's Grave or Llewellyn's Rashness' so exactly evoked a Welsh ballad telling a traditional tale of the noble hound Gelert that people took it to be a genuine Welsh folk-poem. It was set to a Welsh tune and was published 'as sung by the Ancient Britons'. 'Bethgelert', first published in 1800, was included in school anthologies well into the present century, and it is indeed a remarkable work in its evocativeness of a legend still told to tourists who visit Carnarvonshire. King Llewellyn returned to his home to find his child dead, covered in blood which also dripped from the fangs of his hound, who had been left to guard the boy. Rashly, Llewellyn assumes that Gelert has savaged the child, and slays him, only to learn too late, as the faithful dog gives his 'dying yell', that he had been protecting the king's son and fighting off an attacking wolf.

The ballad became immensely popular and was sung in and out of season. This was sometimes a little trying. Playing cards at Panshanger, the home of William Lamb's sister, Lady Cowper, the Princess Lieven, wife of the Russian Ambassador

suddenly gave a start in the middle of a deal. Emily [Lady Cowper's daughter] three rooms off, was vociferating 'Bethgelert': 'Ah! ma chère, le [sic] voilà, cette terrible chanson. Figurez-vous que c'est un chien qui se meurt pendant treize couplets, et je l'ai entendue deux fois et cela fait vingt-six!'[16] *

There are two ways of being a good imitator of literary styles: by being sensitive to the mood of the day, whether it be classicism or romanticism, or by being good at pastiche. Spencer excelled in both. His romantic ballads are poems in their own right, even when they are translations like 'Leonore' or traditional legends like 'Bethgelert'. His English pastiches of fifteenth century French poets, say Charles d'Orleans or even more François Villon, not only followed the contemporary fashion for such imitations, they are delightful in themselves and have the authentic ring of late

---

*Oh, my dear, there's that dreadful song. Just think that it is about a dog which goes on dying during thirteen verses, and I've heard it twice and that makes twenty-six.

C'y gist un povre menestrel,

Occis par maint ennuict cruel—

Ne plains pas trop sa destinée—

N'est icy que son corps mortel;

Son ame est toujours à Gillwell,

Et n'est ce pas là l'Elysée?

One of the poems by William Robert Spencer, from the book published in 1811; opposite is the title page from 'Urania or the Illuminé' by William Spencer which was presented at the Theatre Royal, Drury Lane (British Library).

16

URANIA or the ILLUMINE,

A

New Musical Entertainment,

In Two Acts,

As now Performing with universal applause at the Theatre Royal Drury Lane.

Written by Wm. Spencer Esqr.

The Overture & Music Composed by John Spencer Esqr. & Michael Kelly.

K

To be had of Mr. Kelly at his new Musical Saloon No 9 Pall Mall, with the whole of his Musical Publications & all Foreign supply & Correspondence.

Prd at Platt Hall   Pr.7

medieval French poetry, with all its wistful lyricism and preoccupation with death.

Vain and conceited William Spencer doubtless was — 'he contrived to introduce in the course of the conversation, all the compliments that have ever been paid him . . . for the last twelvemonth',[17] said Harriet Cavendish — but he could take satire directed at himself in good part. *Rejected Addresses,* by Horatio and James Smith, was a collection of verses parodying the leading poets of the day. These in 1812 included Wordsworth, Coleridge, Byron, Scott and Crabbe, as well as William Spencer. The poem of Spencer's chosen for parody was one of his best known, the charming 'To Lady Anne Hamilton':

> Too late I stayed — forgive the crime;
>   Unheeded flew the hours;
> How noiseless falls the foot of time
>   That only treads on flowers.

The Smith brothers included these lines in their parody:

> Ah! whom do my peepers remark?
>   'Tis Hebe with Jupiter's jug;
> Oh no, 'tis the pride of the Park,
>   Fair Lady Elizabeth Mugg.

Most people thought that Spencer would be too hurt and angry to meet the mockers; but when the opportunity occurred, he said that there was no one whom he would be happier to know, and they became firm friends. Byron also reacted generously and wrote from Italy to his publisher Murray that he forgave Smith 'were he twenty times over our satirist'.[18]

As Walter Scott had noted, William Spencer could write fine poetry, and there is indeed, even in some of his light *vers d'occasion*, a haunting feeling of pain remembered and of future uncertainty — both so much part of his own life. He once wrote verses for his wife which he headed 'To Mrs Spencer. On her birthday, with some greenhouse flowers':

> Few, but all thornless, are these flowers,
> The greenhouse saved from wintry showers;
> So memory still in grief retains
> Few joys, but all unmix'd with pains!

May greenhouse sweets remind thee more
Of Springs to come than Summers o'er
Past bliss each present care beguile,
And hope be born from Memory's smile.

Beneath all his facility in German, French and English versifying
was the fact that William was an excellent mimic. The thing that
people most remembered about him was that he was such fun:
'genuine fun in his conversation', Byron said,[19] and many others
wrote of their delight in listening to him. He would tell younger
people, such as John Cam Hobhouse, who was Byron's close friend
and executor, anecdotes about the great politicians he had known.
'Pitt asked Spencer what sort of man Fox was in private
conversation. Fox asked Spencer just the same question of Pitt.'
Fox could on occasion be grumpy and absent-minded. Having
promised Spencer that he would not greet Thomas Moore, the
Irish poet who longed to meet him, by turning his back and saying
humph, 'he did say *humph* and did turn his back directly.'[20] Another
of Spencer's anecdotes was of William Pitt, notoriously chaste in
that unchaste age, who was once persuaded to accompany a group
of friends to a house of ill fame; but Pitt stayed outside in the street
'oratorizing' until they came out again.

Thomas Moore's best story was of Spencer mimicking the
historian Edward Gibbon. A French doctor, Gibbon's rival in the
affections of Lady Elizabeth Foster, was discussing her health with
Gibbon. This was how Spencer used to tell and act it:

'Quand mi lady Elizabeth Foster sera malade de vos fadaises, je la guérirai.'
On which Gibbon, drawing himself up grandly, 'Quand mi lady Elizabeth
Foster sera morte de vos recettes, je l'im-mor-tali-serai.' The pompous
lengthening of the last word, while at the same time a long sustained
pinch of snuff was taken by the historian, brought, as mimicked by
Spencer, the whole scene most livelily before one's eyes.[21]*

His later life was so much overshadowed by debt, unhappiness
and constant recourse to brandy, that it is difficult to put all this
aside and recapture the impression he made in society as a gifted
poet, a man in love with life, and a marvellous raconteur. 'His
singular charm of manner and perhaps of character gave a

---

*When Lady Elizabeth Foster has been made ill by your inanities, I shall cure
her . . . When Lady Elizabeth Foster is dead as a result of your prescriptions, I
shall im-mor-tal-ise her . . .

permanency to his social success by converting the admirers of an evening into friends for life.'[22] The tentative questioning of 'character' in that remark is significant. Men liked him better than women did — was this because he was essentially a dinner-table talker? Charles Fox was reported to have declared — and this was praise indeed — 'that Mr. William Spencer exceeded every man he had ever met with in the happy talent of conversation'.[23] On the other hand, the woman who at that time wrote about him most frequently was his cousin, Lady Harriet Cavendish, and she was then unhappy after the death of her mother, the beloved Duchess Georgiana, and it was during the reign of her father's mistress, Lady Elizabeth Foster, who married the Duke shortly before Harriet herself married. So although Hary-o had a witty tongue, she also had on occasion a cruel and bitter one. 'Brilliant with rouge and spirits . . . William Spencer is staying here and c'est presque tout dire on the disagreeable side . . . He looks like a starved cat, tries one's spirits by his perpetual rattle . . . People say he is brilliant, but I think they must mean noisy . . . '[24]

To most people he was a welcome guest. The restless life, staying in one country house after another, where he was expected to shine and to produce verses always apt for the occasion, the nerve-racking knowledge of mounting debts, had, as so often with Spencer's kind of quick intelligence, a positive side as well. It produced what Madame de Staël called his 'universality', and it appealed to her greatly; she often saw him when she was staying in England, interested as always in constitutional government and meeting everyone in society. She insisted on calling him Robert or Spencer: not that 'low name Guillaume'. Byron on the other hand liked him for different but characteristic reasons: neither his verse nor his conversation were likely to be appreciated by the 'canaille'. There was a good deal of mutual admiration between the older and the younger poet. Spencer thought highly of Byron's poetry and sought his friendship. When Spencer's *Collected Poems* came out in 1811, and on the whole got good reviews, Byron wrote a long critique which, while praising his *vers de société*, yet contained a sharp sting. He mocks the constant use of words like 'gems, roses, birds and diamonds', and — the whole difference between their generations is here, quite apart from Byron's stature as a poet — writes, 'It is happy for the author that these *bijoux* are presented to persons of high degree . . . Lady Blank and Lady Asterisk . . . who are exactly the kind of people to be best pleased with these sparkling, shining, fashionable trifles.'[25]

Between the Irishman Thomas Moore and William Spencer there was genuine affection. They amused each other and shared good times and literary pleasures. When Moore, travelling through the United States and Canada, both of which he much disliked, was homesick and unhappy, he said all this, rather school-boyishly perhaps, in a long poem to Spencer:

> Oh! we had nights of that communion free,
> That flush of heart, which I have known with thee
> So oft, so warmly; nights of mirth and mind,
> Of whims that taught, and follies that refined: . . . [26]

Some of his young admirers thought that Spencer was the only poet of that name. In an amusing letter to Wordsworth, the essayist Charles Lamb describes a conversation with a young man totally at cross purposes: referring to Edmund Spenser and to an exquisite example of a nuptial poem — an epithalamium — on Spenser's own marriage, Charles Lamb was puzzled when his interlocutor asked for the loan of this modern work whose author so excited his admiration, adding, 'Poor Spencer, he has lost his wife.'[27] He was mistaken about that too, thinking no doubt of William Spencer's poem 'The Year of Sorrow' — the year 1804 when many beloved women had died. The Devonshire House circle had died in its essence in 1806: Charles Fox in that year a few months after Georgiana Duchess of Devonshire.

*   *   *   *   *

WOOLBEDING HAD OFFERED the brilliance of the great days of Whig politics. At The Deepdene in Surrey, the home of a rich banker, Thomas Hope, who was himself something of a man of letters, William Spencer was among fellow writers, antiquaries and scientists like his friend Sir Harry Englefield. Gilwell in Essex, the country home of the Chinnery family, gave him music and that which he most needed: true and disinterested friendship.

William Chinnery, like the rich nabob he became after making a fortune as agent in the British colonies, had bought this country estate and begun to entertain very splendidly. The Chinnerys were an interesting family, though accounts of their origins differ; but doubtless Lord Glenbervie spoke for many gossiping and sneering fellow-guests who enjoyed their hospitality but behind their backs said that they 'contrive to purchase the society of all that is most distinguished for rank, beauty, youth, talents, wealth . . . '.[28]

A superficial judgement of this sort did not weigh with William Spencer. The artistic centre which the Chinnery family created still sheds a happy radiance which outshines the snobbery of Glenbervies and the shabbiness of debt which was to fall on many of the people to whom Gilwell was, for a few years, a small paradise. 'Days of joy and gladness' was how the French artist Madame Vigée-Lebrun remembered her visit to Gilwell. The violinist Giovanni Viotti lived with the Chinnerys during all his years in England; Madame Vigée-Lebrun painted a portrait of him; and it is to him that the Chinnerys' concerts largely owe their glow and excitement. Not only was Viotti a great violinist and a superb classical player; he was also experimenting with a new way of playing and is considered the originator of modern techniques.

The Chinnerys' daughter, Caroline, was an exceptionally gifted girl, both as a musician and as a linguist. She had also studied astronomy and mathematics. Spencer's elder daughter Louisa was a friend of hers, and his son William her ardent admirer at the age of twelve. She was quite unspoiled by the fame of her concerts and by her success in society. When only nineteen, she became gravely ill, and stayed in London with the Spencers in order to have the best medical advice; but in less than a year she died.

Well might William Spencer in his troubles recall those days in one of his best Villon-esque verses, and pay a pretty compliment to Gilwell: 'Do not pity this poor minstrel, who died of many a trouble,' for

> N'est ici que son corps mortel;
> Son âme est toujours a Gilwell,
> Et n'est-ce pas là l'Elysée?*

Trouble, financial trouble, was always present. Neither Spencer nor Viotti ever forgot the Chinnerys' kindness to them. Viotti, who was ruined through bad luck rather than through any fault of his,

---

*Only his mortal self lies here;
At Gilwell still his soul remains,
And is not Gilwell Paradise?

suffered great anguish as he was dying because he was unable to repay a debt which he owed to Mrs Chinnery. Spencer was overwhelmed by money and family troubles. By 1810 his family were no longer consistently together; and he was several times in prison for debt, or so the gossip went. Ruined through his own profligacy was the verdict of society. 'I am living with friends,' he wrote, 'the Chinnerys, whose kindness has literally saved my life during two or three years of the greatest possible misery.'[29]

The William Spencers' insolvency had always been common knowledge: after one of the Jenison Walworths' appeals for money, Lady Diana Beauclerk had had to write to Germany that it was out of the question for the Spencers to help, for 'they have not one single shilling but what I believe is lent to him'. Like so many bankrupts, William was eternally hopeful. He rushed into Devonshire House one day, excited because he was to have a share in the management of the Theatre Royal, Drury Lane. He collected his poems together into a small volume on the promise of £200 from his publisher. Earlier, as his family increased, he had taken a permanent government post as Commissioner for Stamps. It was drudgery, and he admitted that colleagues were good enough to cover his frequent absences. While he was there, he used at least some of the time — and government stationery, doubtless — to compose verses. Miss Mary Bouverie was the recipient of a birthday poem written in these circumstances. This young lady also had the honour of a birthday letter from the Secretary of State, Mr Fox. But these were light-hearted moments in the deepening gloom of William's life.

Like his cousins Georgiana Duchess of Devonshire and Lady Bessborough, like his friend Charles Fox, like in fact everybody in that Devonshire House society, the web of debt into which they entangled themselves became for all of them a stifling pall. There was no drawing back. One debt was used to pay off another; dignity and integrity were trampled as each one borrowed from friend or relation, banker, servant, tradesman or money lender. William Spencer turned to the young Duke of Devonshire for assistance, and was rarely if ever refused. Like every debtor and gambler who has been helped, his gratitude was exuberant: '10000000000 thanks for your invaluable kindness, I never can owe so much to any human being as to *you*, . . .'[30] he wrote to the Duke in 1820; and two years later the usual optimism came bubbling up — one more loan to raise an annuity will settle everything: ' . . . . I shall be free and *when free*, have quite income enough for further expenses.'[31]

The year 1825 was one of grave danger for the national economy, and William Spencer was only one among many to be broken by it. The money market was in a critical state; the value of shares fell; the foreign exchange rate turned against this country; and the papers published long lists of bankruptcies. Spencer, unable to meet his creditors, became what was euphemistically called 'a voluntary exile' and left England for good. He had foreseen and feared this possibility. It was not all extravagance that caused his final ruin; his family responsibilities, and particularly the troubles of his daughter Harriet since 1817, with the birth of her child Susan in 1818, as well as his sons' education, were as he said 'inevitable' causes of bankruptcy. He put it clearly to the Duke of Devonshire in May 1822:

 . . . I conclude that Mrs. Spencer has told you something of our situation, expenses *inevitable* and *growing out of other sad domestic misfortunes* for these last three or four years have made it impossible for me not to contract debts, which *now must* be paid, or I *must* give up either my *liberty* or my *country*, and in either case must *lose my official situation*, the salary of which is the chief part of our support.[32]

Spencer spent the remaining nine years of his life in Paris. His friend Chinnery, who was one of the Clerks to the Treasury, defaulted on his own debts and also fled the country. Eventually, in a curious parallel with Spencer's life, he settled in Paris and died there the same year.

*   *   *   *   *

ALTHOUGH THEY ENTERTAINED, and went into society together, William and Susan Spencer's lives were largely spent separately, in movement and restlessness. Spencer is 'in lodgings', or living with the Chinnerys, or in the country houses of the different circles in which he moved — bankers and artists on the one hand, or houses like Chatsworth or Roehampton on the other. Mrs Spencer also is glimpsed staying with people but — except in the early years when she sometimes went to Woolbeding during and after her pregnancies, or when they were all recovering from scarlet fever — rarely accompanied by her husband or children.

Mrs Spencer had been beautiful, and could be very amiable; but the personality that has come down to us is without charm or grace. She had irritating mannerisms: for instance at a Devonshire House dinner she was seen 'acting nine years old with great success'.[33] That she was unfaithful to her husband there can be no doubt; she was not only more indiscreet but more promiscuous than was usual among ladies of fashion, for most of the Devonshire House ladies maintained a certain faithfulness to their lovers. The indiscretion was by far the more unforgivable offence. Her name was linked with several men, including her husband's friend Sir Harry Englefield, and even with the old Duke of Devonshire — though this rumour originated with the Princess Caroline of Wales and she was notorious for getting things wrong and for telling anecdotes about the unchastity of all the women she knew.[34] She said that Mrs Spencer had taken the place formerly held by Lady Elizabeth Foster, now herself Duchess of Devonshire.

So blatant was her conduct that her husband said, whether in a jest in bad taste or in the earnestness of despair was not clear, that the two youngest children were not his. Their father was alleged to be J.W. Ward, Lord Dudley. Indeed, as far as the youngest of the six children was concerned, there can be no question of allegation about it, for the fact is that in a codicil to his Will, dated 1831, Dudley left £25,000 to Frederick Spencer. The name by which young Frederick had been known in Devonshire House circles gives a sad and revealing insight into the Spencers' family life. He was called 'the Forsaken'.[35]

In a second codicil Lord Dudley left Mrs Spencer an annuity of £800; it was to be for her 'separate use and independent of her present or any future husband'.[36]

Lord Dudley was singled out by the Princess Lieven, when she was discussing various politicians, as an honourable man. His provision for Mrs Spencer, and for the boy to whom in his will he referred as the son of William Spencer, as well as an annuity for another of his women friends, confirm that this exceedingly rich bachelor behaved with propriety in such matters. He was esteemed by his friends for a kind man, though many people found his conversation coarse and his table manners disgusting. John Hobhouse defined the feeling of uncertainty about Lord Dudley when he wrote that 'there is something kind and attentive, but rather unquiet, in his manner':[37] These were early signs of his deteriorating mental state, for he died insane. Caroline Lamb brought him into her novel *Glenarvon* as Lord Dallas.

Even her husband's friend Mr Hope did not conceal his dislike of Mrs Spencer's 'avarice and shabby begging . . . '; he described this really horrible scene which had taken place in his house: 'Mrs Spencer began by talking in raptures of a certain remarkably fine ruby ring which Sir Harry Englefield wore. "Mama" said her son [this was the youngest, Frederick] in an ironical tone "Could you not get it from him you who get so many things from him? . . . " "And if I did" cried the mother coloring with anger and outraged beyond her prudence "And if I did Sir it should not be for you."'[38]

When the Spencers' marriage finally broke up, Mrs Spencer went to live in Germany, where at least one of her sons kept in touch with her. She lived only about seven years to enjoy Lord Dudley's annuity.

This then was the unhappy, restless, worldly family in which the Spencer children grew up. Some of them reacted to the raffishness by becoming eminently respectable: two of the boys were ordained and eventually became bishops overseas in an expanding British Empire; and Louisa became a devout Roman Catholic. But for the younger daughter Harriet the lack of guidance and support from her father, her mother's example and conduct, and no doubt the endless movement and instability and financial insecurity of this disordered family led to tragedy.

The tragedy for Harriet was not so much the fact of her seduction — unmarried girls in high society were after all sometimes seduced — as the publicity which surrounded it. Harriet was unusual for her time and her class in that she had behaved in such a manner as publicly to acquire a bad reputation. She frequented the company of young unmarried men, such as Henry de Ros, who were notorious for an extravagant and profligate life. Mrs Arbuthnot, the Duke of Wellington's friend, who kept a sharp eye on the social scene and noted it all in her journal, said of Mr (later Lord) de Ros: 'he is the most disgusting mass of affectation I ever saw in my life. He puts on an appearance of *softness & modesty* such as one never saw, & is in reality the most profligate good for nothing man in the Kingdom.'[39] The signal failure of Harriet's parents to protect her reputation is evident in the dreadful and unusual fact that the men in that company of young people themselves bandied her name about. For the older generation, a girl in polite society to whom this happened was forever degraded. Gentlemen, among themselves, had always of course told of their conquests of young girls or of well-known courtesans; but to repeat publicly what appears to have been the disorderly behaviour of poor Harriet was so shocking that Sir Harry Englefield, a close friend of the Spencers, wrote to the Duke of Devonshire of his distress at all 'these reports which must I fear have arisen from the indiscretion (though that is *not* the proper word) of those men whose lips should have been the last to be ever opened on the subject. If it be so, I want words to express my abhorrence of their conduct.'[40]

It was this public aspect of the case which so scandalised society and led to the ostracising of the Spencers and all the mixed feelings at the ball which, two years after the birth of Susan, the Duke of Devonshire gave for Harriet. Harriet had admitted to her mother to an association with Mr de Ros, and to great imprudence in her conduct to Mr Wombwell, who had been an exact contemporary at Eton and in the same form as George Spencer-Churchill, in 1817 Marquis of Blandford. It must be recognised here that Susan Churchill learnt of her paternity only at the time of or even after her marriage, and that the name of George Spencer-Churchill does not appear in the gossip surrounding Harriet and this group of young men; and that for reasons which become clearer later a complete conspiracy of silence hid the fact of Susan's birth and her paternity from this time on. To all appearances, Harriet Spencer's parents behaved, after Susan's birth in March 1818, as if the baby did not exist.

Early in 1818 Spencer gave up the house in Curzon Street and went to live in Sir Harry Englefield's house at Petersham, near Richmond in Surrey. Soon afterwards, he spent a few months in Germany. In Darmstadt the Elector of Hesse decorated him with an order. That, however, was not the sole purpose of his journey. Links with the German side of his wife's family had continued through the years, and marriages with other German families had added numbers of cousins, among whom were the von Westerholts, counts of the Holy Roman Empire, originally from Westphalia.

When the calamity of Harriet's seduction struck them, the Spencers were plunged into the greatest unhappiness and misery. William's wit was dimmed for a time, and Sir Harry Englefield found Mrs Spencer 'most wretched & most anxious to clear her daughters character . . . [41] of at least some of the worst imputations of gossips. She was writing to the Duke of Devonshire when the news of Susan's birth came, and most dramatically she breaks off in mid-sentence, and then continues:

I had written thus far when the event I have been so long expecting took place, and which has affected me as much as if I never had expected it, & put it completely out of my power to continue the details I wish'd to give . . . [42]

That is the last reference to Susan ever to be traced to her nearest relations, but for Harriet the Spencers began to entertain the hope of marriage with her cousin Charles von Westerholt. Her father's negotiations proved successful, and in April 1819, Mrs Spencer was writing to the Duke of Devonshire:

Petersham — April 8th 1819

At last my dearest duke I have the happiness to be able to tell you that Harriet is going to be married to the Count Charles de Westerholdt — a match in every way delightful to us — "Les Convenances et l'Amour se trouvent d'accord". It was a marriage I wish'd for ever since I first went to Germany but I never dared hope Ct Wt the Father would have consented — however on knowing Harrio thoroughly he is so much pleased with her character and the young people are so much in love that he has consented & they are to be married immediately — there is but one drawback to my happiness it is which is [sic] his making a point of their living in Germany as he says he can not think of depriving himself of the society of his only son — all he can do for me is to allow them to come & see us soon after their marriage for six weeks.

I feel *quite* certain that this news will give you pleasure — God bless you my dear duke — *When* shall you return? I do want very very much to see you again.[43]

Charles von Westerholt and Harriet Spencer were married at Ratisbon (Regensburg), in Bavaria, in October 1819. The account given in Mrs Spencer's letter of the attitude of Count von Westerholt *père* varies considerably from what was being said about the match in England. According to widespread reports at home, the von Westerholts were told about the birth of Harriet's child, but not about her public disgrace. It was thought that the publicity had not penetrated beyond London society, and that once again the name of Spencer had cast its spell over the German family. The Count, wrote Miss Edgeworth, asked no questions and was only too happy to be 'connected with the great Duke of Marlborough's family'.

Then in April 1820, the Duke of Devonshire, in the kindness of his heart, gave the ball for Harriet and her husband. It was a gesture of friendship in the grand manner to the William Spencers, and a bold challenge by the young Duke to the hypocrisy of society, who had ostracised Harriet less for what she had done than for having been found out. 'We got to London early,' Mrs Arbuthnot recorded in her diary, '& went at night to a ball given by the Duke of Devonshire at Chiswick. It was very fine but not very gay & the occasion of its being given kept many persons away'. Count Charles' father, Mrs Arbuthnot goes on, had refused to make a settlement unless Harriet were received once more into English society. 'She and her husband accordingly came, & the Duke of Devonshire gave this grand ball, to which most of the town went; but, as no one spoke to her, I do not see that it will assist much in patching up her broken reputation.'

All this is unbearably painful, and it comes as a relief to read Mrs Spencer's next letter to the Duke of Devonshire. Although she was inevitably putting on a brave face, and unintentionally reveals that Charles von Westerholt's father had not easily accepted his daughter-in-law, her news of the birth of a boy to Charles and Harriet and of their home in Germany does to some extent compensate for the cruel rejection by society in England:

[*Endorsed* 23rd Oct. 1820]

. . . I had a letter the other day from Ratisbonn that made me very happy — if it was not in German I should like to send it to you — it is from my sister with an account of all Ct West: has been doing for the reception of Carl and Harrio — amongst other things that he has had a Cradle made for his little grand son that is the admiration of all the *mothers* in Ratisbonn — & that he had fitted up those rooms for Harrio's private appartment [sic] with every comfort & ornament he could procure.

All this shows him so completely reconciled to the marriage that it makes me very very happy indeed . . .

And now if you are bored with all these details [about a portrait of the Duke which her sister wanted] only remember that you have drawn them on yourself by yr kindness — a bad return you will say — but I do not believe you will say so — And so God keep you my dear dear duke . . . [44]

Harriet was still 'contented and happy' at the end of 1821 when, the Duke noted in his diary after hearing from Mrs Spencer, she and her husband returned to England 'to pass 3 or 4 quiet months at Petersham'.[45] Miss Edgeworth was therefore misled by the gossip which would have had Harriet 'living in some obscure lodging in London' in 1822 — but gossip there still was. From then on the young Westerholts disappear from the scene. Harriet's brother, the Rev. George Trevor Spencer, never lost touch with all the Westerholt cousins, later arranging for their visits to England, and seeing them when he himself visited his mother in Mannheim. Mrs Spencer's health deteriorated in the last years of her life, which ended about five years after her husband's.

A few months before William Spencer's death in Paris, in 1834, his biographer and friend, Miss Poulter, said that he 'received the account of the death of a very dear relation which greatly distressed him — then a letter saying this person "had for some years led an exemplary life". He exclaimed, Thank God for this! . . . I have heard the only thing that is of consequence *now*.' Susan Churchill thought that her mother had died in 1835, but she was not sure of the date. Miss Poulter's discreet words betray no confidence that may have been placed in her by Spencer; nevertheless they almost certainly mark the end of Harriet's life. Her sister Louisa constantly afterwards prayed for the repose of her soul.

Before William Spencer was forced into exile by his debts, his conversation was becoming strident and his fun brittle. Unhappiness is a destructive force, and William was a shell of his earlier self. Yet there is an element of courage in his bearing, in being '*professionally* the enlivener of every dinner and every party . . .'[46] Sad to say, friends who used to enjoy his company now preferred dinner parties without him. He had lost his spontaneous gaiety and was trying too hard to be witty. His young daughter-in-law found his visits 'intolerable'. They were indeed hard on her furniture:

. . . he relishes nothing and finds fault with every thing covers the carpets and sofa with snuff, drinks between 2 and 3 bottles of wine a day besides brandy and *snaps* at every thing George says. What an amiable character I have given of him![47]

Tales of ageing, shabby English gentlemen trying to keep up appearances in their exile in Paris are all too familiar, in fiction and in fact. William Spencer's was one of the sadder ones. He received visits from two of his sons and their wives, and he occasionally went into society, though hardly as the 'lion' of former days, as Miss Poulter believed, but more probably as a wretched old man on its fringe. Miss Poulter was proud when he went to meet Walter Scott; Scott himself wrote of that occasion, 'Another gloomy day . . . I expect RWS [sic] to breakfast. There is another thought which depresses me.'[48]

Spencer's was a complex character, with a streak of weakness which allowed his life to be blighted. He was capable of friendship, but warm, secure family love escaped him. He gave no sign of being fond of children; rather the opposite in the view of those who knew him well. He could, nonetheless, imbue his verse with sheer fun for young people, as in his poem 'To a Grammatical Niece':

> The *Nom'native* which I study's — "*a Niece,*"
>   Who is *genitive* ever of kindness to me;
> When I'm sad she's so *Dative* of comfort and peace,
>   That I scarce against fate can *Accusative* be.
> O Friendship (this *Vocative* most I prefer)
>   Make my case always *Ablative* — by and with her . . . [49]

He met the spirit of late eighteenth and early nineteenth century society at its most superficial level, and endeavoured to amuse it: in this he was successful. Yet some of his verse does not deserve the oblivion in which it is lost, and he showed that he knew the meaning of sorrow, of broken hope, and of love. 'Epitaph on Miss Spencer' was written on the death of his niece, John Spencer's daughter. 'The Year of Sorrow' begins with the feelings of a daughter unavoidably absent from her mother's death bed:

> Ah! no — whilst others watched thy ebbing breath,
> And lightened by their love the load of death, . . .

Lockhart was intolerably harsh in judging Miss Poulter a 'weak silly *fade* old spinster', for underneath the fashionable panegyric style of her memoir (which William Spencer himself had used on occasion), Miss Poulter may have been describing in his last years the real man whom she knew and revered: an older, wiser William Spencer who perhaps had come to a deeper understanding of life. Certainly he was fortunate in having at the end the company of one who rightly called herself his 'winter-friend'.[50]

31

NOTES

1. *The Glenbervie Journals,* edited by Walter Sichel.
2. *Notes and Queries,* Vol 187, 'Some Unpublished Letters of J. G. Lockhart'.
3. *Life of Sir Walter Scott,* J. G. Lockhart.
4. *Georgiana. Extracts from the Correspondence of Georgiana, Duchess of Devonshire,* edited by The Earl of Bessborough.
5. Lord Granville Leveson Gower, *Private Correspondence 1781 to 1821,* edited by Castalia Countess Granville.
6. *Miss Eden's Letters,* edited by Violet Dickinson.
7. *The Life of Charles James Fox,* E. C. P. Lascelles.
8. *Georgiana.*
9. *Recollections of a Long Life,* Lord Broughton (John Cam Hobhouse).
10. *Letters from 1797 to 1807,* letters from Lady Diana Beauclerk to her daughter Countess Mary Jenison Walworth, printed by J. Hoerning, Heidelberg. (I am indebted to Mrs A. E. Duncan-Jones for the loan of this small collection of letters, printed privately in Germany, circa 1930.)
11. Lord Granville Leveson Gower, op. cit.
12. Lord Glenbervie (Sichel), op. cit.
13. William Robert Spencer's Preface to his opera *Urania or The Illuminé.*
14. Lady Diana Beauclerk, op. cit.
15. Memorial tablet in Woolbeding Church, Sussex.
16. *Letters of Harriet Countess Granville, 1810-1845,* edited by The Hon. F. Leveson Gower.
17. *Hary-o. The Letters of Lady Harriet Cavendish, 1796-1809,* edited by Sir George Leveson Gower.
18. *Rejected Addresses,* The Brothers Horatio and James Smith. First published in 1812.
19. Quoted by Miss Louisa Poulter in her *Memoir* from *Conversations of Lord Byron with the Countess Blessington.*
20. Lord Broughton, op. cit.
21. *Memoirs, Journal and Correspondence of Thomas Moore,* edited by Lord John Russell.
22. *Recollections of a Literary Life,* Mary Russell Mitford.
23. *The Satirist or Monthly Meteor,* 1 Dec. 1811.
24. *Hary-o.*
25. *Monthly Review,* Vol. 67, Jan. 1812, review of *Poems* by William Robert Spencer. Unsigned but identified by L. A. Marchand in his edition of Byron's *Letters* as being by Byron.

26. *The Poetical Works of Thomas Moore*, from Epistle VIII of Epistles, Odes and other Poems.

27. *The Works of Charles and Mary Lamb*, edited by E. V. Lucas, Vol. VI, Letters, 1796-1820.

28. Lord Glenbervie (Sichel), op. cit.

29. Hist. MSS Commission 30 Fortescue X. W. R. Spencer to Thomas Grenville.

30. Devonshire MSS, Chatsworth, 6th Duke's Group, 436.

31, 32. ibid., 639.

33. Harriet Countess Granville, op. cit.

34. *The Diaries of Sylvester Douglas, Lord Glenbervie,* edited by Francis Bickley.

35. Devonshire MSS, 2741.1. Lady Carlisle to Lady Granville, March 1833.

36. Public Record Office. Will of the Earl of Dudley, Sept. 566-1833. Also *Creevey,* edited by John Gore.

37. Lord Broughton, op. cit.

38. *Maria Edgeworth. Letters from England, 1813-1844,* edited by Christina Colville.

39. *The Journal of Mrs Arbuthonot,* edited by Francis Bamford and the Duke of Wellington.

40, 41. Devonshire MSS, 285

42. ibid., 304.

43. ibid.,351.

44. ibid., 461.

45. ibid., 767.445, 1821.9.

46. Maria Edgeworth, op. cit.

47. British Library Add. MSS, Broughton Papers, 36,460 f.262: Mrs George Trevor Spencer to her brother, John Cam Hobhouse [undated].

48. *Journal of Sir Walter Scott,* edited by W. E. K. Anderson.

49. *The Satirist or Monthly Meteor,* 1 Dec. 1811.

50. From the only poem by Louisa Poulter included in her *Memoir of W. R. Spencer.*

CHAPTER TWO

Brocket Hall

I hear you received the Queen at Brockett — I should
like to have been hid among the trees to see you all pass
— I hope Her Majesty was pleased with dear old
Brockett?

letter from Susan to Lord Melbourne, 1841[1]

WHEN HARRIET SPENCER was a girl, there was a kind
of moral cynicism abroad in fashionable society. It was superficial,
as all such trends are: family values usually abide, even underneath
the fluttering romances of a Devonshire House. 'A Key to Modern
Polite Conversation',[2] which appeared in several magazines around
1818, describes this cynicism in a light parody:

Truth: memory uncertain. Matrimony: a blind bargain, wherein a
fashionable man and wife revolve like the sun and moon, *shunning* and
eclipsing each other. At Home: a domestic circle of 300 visitors. Husband: a
domestic animal, legally authorised to pay a wife's debts. Debt: a
necessarily genteel evil. Duty: doing like other people, drinking, gaming,
wenching. Morality: a troublesome interrupter of pleasure . . .

and so on.

Even if a girl had a mother anxious to protect her daughter's
reputation, as Harriet clearly had not, the position of women in
high society and the whole social pattern frequently reduced such
protection to no more than vigilant bargaining in the marriage
market. That devoted mother, William Lamb's sister, Lady
Cowper, wrote continually to their brother Frederick, listing
possible matches for her daughter and describing girls who might
tempt Frederick to matrimony. Gossip in drawing rooms dwelt
much on how families should conduct themselves when an
unmarried daughter had the misfortune to become pregnant. At
all costs the fact must be concealed, the girl delivered of her child

in some remote place, if possible abroad, and the child kept out of sight. Then the girl must be married as soon as possible: the difficulty of finding a husband was much discussed, because it was considered wrong to keep the man in the dark about what had happened. Above all, the birth must be kept secret and no *public* knowledge of the event must be allowed. Unlike the illegitimate children of married women, the child of an unmarried girl must remain invisible and unknown. Except for the last, the William Spencers had failed in all these criteria; consequently they were despised and Harriet's life was, in the true sense of the word, ruined. As the *Key* put it: 'Vice: only applied to horses and men servants'.

Fortunately for Susan, her mother Harriet Spencer had spent much of her time with her older cousin Lady Bessborough, who was greatly concerned when Harriet's condition became known. There were family conferences, in which their friend Sir Harry Englefield took part, and it appears to have been decided that at birth the baby would disappear from the circle of her close relations and become the responsibility of Lady Bessborough.

In later life Susan was told that she had been born in London, thus already creating a difference between her life and that of other children of unmarried mothers, who in these circles were generally born abroad. It is of course possible that Susan was born in Germany where her mother eventually married; but this is unlikely, because William Spencer left for Germany in 1818 only after May, Susan having been born in March. Also there is little doubt that Lady Bessborough, from the day of Susan's birth of which the circumstances were successfully concealed, whisked her away to the Bessborough house at Roehampton near Richmond in Surrey.

Lady Bessborough had some experience in the concealment of socially awkward pregnancies. Her sister Georgiana Devonshire was already the mother of her three legitimate children when she conceived Charles Grey's child. Henrietta Bessborough was at that time recovering from a serious illness; she persuaded her doctor to send her abroad to convalesce and to advise the companionship of her sister Georgiana, whose husband the Duke of Devonshire suspected the truth. They went to Europe together for a considerable time, during which Charles Grey's daughter was born to Georgiana.

Susan's first three years were spent at Roehampton, and she

lived her childhood years mainly at Brocket Hall, the favourite home of the Melbournes, in Hertfordshire. Home therefore for Susan was always where the Ponsonbys — the Bessborough family — or where William and Caroline Lamb — particularly of course Caroline — were living or staying.

The child was nearing her fourth year when Lady Bessborough died, and it is doubtful whether she remembered that first 'mother', who was also her godmother.

Henrietta Ponsonby, Countess of Bessborough, is almost intimately known to us through her own letters and those of her family and friends. In spite of her detractors — mostly Byron's champions when she stood by her daughter Caroline Lamb during the Byron affair and was driven distracted by worry, but also those who took for affectation or hypocrisy the soft Devonshire House lisp — the feeling that she still evokes is one of affection. She was good, kind and devout; extravagant; a fond but unfaithful wife though a faithful lover; a most loving mother, whose children were 'passionately attached to her'[3]; not always wise; impulsive and warm; compassionate and yet sometimes curiously insensitive as she proved when she encouraged the marriage of her niece Harriet Cavendish to her own lover, Lord Granville Leveson Gower — though as it happened that marriage turned out to be ideally happy. She cannot lightly have broken her marriage vows, and she had thought deeply about the condition of women. In her views on unmarried mothers, she is in some respects a surprising

OPPOSITE:

This charming sketch, which has lain all these years among Lord Bessborough's papers, can be said with practical certainty to be by Caroline Lamb. The paper on which it is drawn is folded round a number of poems written by her, some of them, like 'The Waters of Elle', being clearly early versions of poems which were published later. Although the identities of the young girl and the child in the sketch are unknown, the drawing illustrates the theme of this book, so much of which concerns childhood at Brocket in the last years of Caroline Lamb's life and the effects of that upbringing on Susan.

From her clothes and stance, the older girl appears to be a nursemaid, and she is refusing to do or to give something which the child wants. The drawing is characteristic of those which Caroline Lamb used to sketch on odd scraps of paper and send to her correspondents.

forerunner of that famous Victorian fighter against what came to be called the double moral standard for men and women, Josephine Butler. When she took her young cousin Harriet Spencer's baby into her family, she was not only behaving in the spontaneous ways of her circle in adding another child to her establishment; she was, it is fair to assume, putting consciously held principles into practice. Yet the sound ethical sentiments which she expresses show the confusion of thought of her time: she is unaware that she is advocating one standard of conduct for unmarried and another for married women like herself. The end of her letter also raises a slight suspicion that she is thinking here of girls from a world outside the small, usually protected, circle of the Harriet Spencers. Nevertheless this is a bold and thoughtful statement:

So far from thinking breach of Chastity and Morals should go unpunish'd [she had written sixteen years earlier to Lord Granville Leveson Gower], they ought to be discouraged in every possible way as much from *compassion* as from justice, for to a woman . . . the almost constant consequence is sinking into the lowest state of degradation. But the great fault I find in all trials [i.e. judgements] of this sort is the favour men are inclin'd to show to one another, reserving all the severity for the victims — the Mother and the child. Were the punishment very severe for the Man . . . and provision made for the child it would save many vices in discouraging one; but as it is, the man escapes with a trifling punishment and no disgrace, the poor Girl is expos'd to so much scorn and Taunting, the child so ill taken care of . . . that one can hardly be surprised . . . [if] some poor creatures [should be tempted] to destroy their offspring either before or immediately after their coming into the world.[4]

Frederick Ponsonby, third Earl of Bessborough, has often seemed a shadowy figure behind his wife's brilliant appearance in society, or her worries over their daughter Caroline — perhaps a complaisant husband and altogether rather a dull man. Harriet Cavendish, visiting Roehampton, dismissed him as 'foolish beyond permission', with a 'childish ill-humour, quite insupportable.'[5] Lord Hartington thought that his aunt Henrietta had married Frederick Ponsonby not for love nor because he was particularly brilliant but because it was expected of her and Ponsonby was an eligible *parti*. However that may have been, the world in general esteemed and respected Lord Bessborough. 'He had an instinctive knowledge of mankind, and his manners being very pleasing and his understanding very good, though not of the higher order, he was an agreeable and a welcome companion wherever he went.'[6] He plays an important part in Susan's story, and his happy understanding of children is vividly present in the letters which he wrote to his grandson Augustus Lamb — letters such as to interest that poor retarded boy but never to condescend to him. He rarely forgets Susan in the letters, and regularly sends his love. There are messages for her about a doll, or about her prayer-book which had been left at Melbourne House in Whitehall. When, after Caroline Lamb's death, Susan spends her school holidays in the care of a housekeeper, he shows in a few words in the news he gives of her to Augustus an understanding compassion for the lonely child.

Caroline Lamb was strongly maternal. Her joy and pleasure in her baby son Augustus shine through the accounts of her friends and family — 'Caro's boy and her rapture at its birth' — though when Harriet Cavendish saw the small infant for the first time, she made a prescient observation about his 'odd helpless countenance'.[7] As, gradually, Caroline and William Lamb came to realise his mental abnormality and to dread his epileptic attacks, his mother persevered in her care for him, writing to him when he was away with his tutor or during her own frequent absences, and adapting her letters to his childish understanding, while trying to guide and prepare him for a maturity which never came.[8]

Like her mother, Caroline thought it a matter of course to have a household of children for whom she assumed some degree of responsibility. A few months before Lady Bessborough's death in Italy, Caroline wrote to her: 'We leave town, thank Heaven, Monday, & I propose taking Frederic Sysonby with me to Brocket for a time in order to see what is best to be done with him about a school. I also take the infant again, but not as a clog, only for a little amusement & air.'[9] The date of this letter makes it almost certain that the infant was Susan. Earlier, she had looked after another child, Russell, an illegitimate son of the Duke of Bedford, whom she called her *petit* friend and had nursed 'when he was but three'.[10]

When, therefore, Caroline suffered the loss of her greatly loved mother, and Susan that of her godmother, there seemed no question but that the child should continue to live as a member of the family. She also to some extent filled a void: so far, the Lambs had no daughter. A girl had been born early in 1820, but had lived only a few hours, to Caroline's grief. To have a little girl running about the drawing-room at Brocket, wearing a sash round her frock and a coral necklace, brought some simple pleasure to both William and Caroline, which William was to remember later.

Susan was not a lonely child at Brocket, for there were a number of children of varying ages in and around the place. The succession of doctors engaged to care for Augustus and Lady Caroline brought their families with them. Susan played with their children. There was 'little James Roe', the son of Dr G.H. Roe who sometimes wrote Caroline's letters for her (her life-long habit of dictating letters had always been deplored by her mother), and there was 'little Mary at the stable' of whom Augustus was so fond. Dr Goddard's wife was much gratified at the way her son had been received at Roehampton, and, very shortly before she died, Caroline reported to his parents that the Crosby boy was 'very entertaining and well'.[11]

Clearly Susan, though not isolated, led a secluded life and did not meet children who were her social equals, except for a few, like Fanny Ponsonby, Lord Bessborough's grandchild, who was almost the same age as Susan. There is no evidence that she knew William Lamb's nephews, the Cowper children at Panshanger, only a few miles from Brocket.

During her childhood, Susan knew two sets of adults. On the one hand, the aristocratic circle of Ponsonbys, Lambs, even a friend of her real parents, came and went, though she seems never to have known her own parents nor her Spencer grandparents. Old Lord Melbourne, William Lamb's father, vegetated quietly at Brocket; he was fond of Susan, Caroline thought, and he must at least have provided in all the turmoil of Lamb family life the stability of someone who was always there.

On the other hand, Caroline Lamb possessed the gift of transcending social hierarchies and of seeing people in human terms; she brought her vitality and imagination into any company. In the past this had amazed her relations: 'Caro [at Cowes] . . . leading the sort of life people do in a Harlequin farce, perpetual shifting of scene, dress and company, lodging at an apothecary's, dining at the Duke of Gloucester's, enfant de famille at Mrs. Knox's, an Irish lady who gives assemblies in London, one minute on a Pillion, the next in a boat . . . '[12] There are echoes of this unselfconscious casualness in Susan's girlhood years in Geneva.

Susan would have been familiar with the train of people employed by the Lambs: the succession of doctors, Lee, Roe,

Account from Evans & Rawlins of Oxford Street for items for Susan, paid for through Mrs Peterson (Panshanger MSS).

paid for Susan

Gloves & Stockings	0 . 16 . 3
Pocket hand.f & pincushion	0 . 6 . 8
Miss Giles — —	1 . 19 . 6
white — —	0 . 10 . 3
Bonnet —	0 . 12 . 0
Mrs Raven —	0 . 18 . 10
washing —	0 . 10 . 0
Miss Munk —	1 . 18 . 0
present to Children	1 . 0 . 0
present to Susan	0 . 12 . 0
	£ 9 . 2 . 6
received —	£ 6 . 0 . 0
remains due	£ 3 . 2 . 6
to Mrs P	
	0 — 5 — 0
W Dukes —	3 . 7 . 6

Tradesman's account for drapery items including gloves, stockings, bonnet, and pocket hankerchiefs, supplied for Susan and paid for through Mrs Peterson (Panshanger MSS).

Account for 'Instructing Miss Susan Half a quarter to Christmas' (1827) rendered by Susan's school mistress, Miss Monk, and including sundries like 'Sampler & silk' and 'Spelling book', with a note to say 'School will be open on 21st of Jany'. The account was paid on January 10, 1828 (Panshanger MSS).

Goddard; the housekeepers, particularly Mrs Peterson when she visited Brocket from Roehampton or London; Susan's Roehampton nurse, Mrs Thomson; and women such as Miss Fanny Richardson, Miss Webster, Miss Rosina Wheeler (who married the novelist Lord Lytton), Miss Mortimer, who all appear in undefined roles round Lady Caroline, writing her letters, running errands, managing the household, or looking after Augustus. She may well have known the splendidly named *chef* Mr Napoleon, referred to in the household accounts as Mr Napoleon de Paris.

The staff at Brocket, according to Caroline's sister-in-law Lady Cowper, was not particularly happy and relied on long-standing members like the steward Hagard to run the establishment with some semblance of order. To a child, however, eccentricity and upheaval are normal if that is all she has known. There is only one servant whom Susan is on record as having hated — one Robert whom William Lamb later dismissed, but only after she had left Brocket. The child's strong feeling suggests certainly impertinent, and possibly cruel, behaviour on his part.

Mrs Peterson was particularly important to the whole family and to Susan. She had been Lady Bessborough's maid for nearly forty years, and she became the Ponsonbys' London housekeeper. She it was who had written the often quoted anguished and reproachful letter to Caroline on the famous occasion when, knowing that she had lost all hold on Byron, Caroline ran away and hid. Lady Bessborough had been made seriously ill by this episode — hence the letter. Mrs Peterson had known Susan since her birth, and when Lady Caroline died, she took charge of her, continued to buy her clothes, accounted for any money that was spent on the child, and looked after her during her school holidays.

Susan had known Augustus Lamb all her life. She was eleven years younger, but his mental age was such that, as the toddler grew into a little girl during seven years at Brocket, they remained contemporary play-fellows. They were devoted to each other and if one were away from Brocket the other wrote or sent messages. Susan seems to have had a child's instinctive acceptance of Augustus' disability; and, as she progressed normally in learning to read and write, to show an intuitive understanding of his slowness. By the time she was nine years old, she was writing to him in a clear script, sometimes on carefully ruled lines, rather as an adult might write to a child so that he may read the letter himself, and not in her, at that time, already fairly mature hand:

My Dear Augustus
    as you liked my silver pen so much I am qu[i]te willing to change it for
your silver pencil. Now you are learning to write, you can write me a nice
letter. I am ashamed of this, but it is the fault of my ink. Pray give my love
to Bell [one of the dogs] and all other enquiring Friends.

                                                    yours affectionately
Jan 26th 1827   Susan [13]

Miss Fanny Richardson, with a rather tasteless coyness, wrote to
Augustus about 'your little wife Susan' who was working at her
arithmetic which she was anxious to be good at. She did in fact
later show a good understanding of financial matters.
    Meanwhile Augustus' physical growth outstripped the
development of his mind. His aunt Lady Cowper's description of
him has been much quoted: the great strong eighteen-year-old
young man frightening the housemaids out of their wits by
jumping at them and rolling on them. His mother tried to get him
to abandon his 'bad Tricks . . . such pinching of people & dogs
and such other Idle habits . . . '[14] All this must inevitably have
caused anxiety to those who were responsible for Susan; but there
is no suggestion that Augustus ever treated her with anything but
gentleness and brotherly affection. Even for her young age, she
was very small, and it is probable that the boy who had known and
been fond of the child since her birth was in no way aroused by
her either sexually or to a playful roughness. But for Susan, it
became clear later that her childhood spent largely with boys had
given her, for her times, both a frankness with men that was
endearing but also an unconventional tomboyishness. In any case,
the boisterousness of the Lambs, and of William in particular, had
long been notorious, and would have been accepted by Susan as
normal social behaviour.
    The childhood years at Brocket were happy and full. There were
occasional holidays by the sea. Lady Caroline and Susan wrote
almost identical letters to Augustus describing their house on a hill
at Hastings.[15] Susan's is, for her, ill-spelt and badly written, with the
lines wandering all over the page; but it must be one of her earliest
letters when she was a very small child.

Dear Augustus
to Day at Hastings has been beautiful the sands and beach crowded with
People I wish you were hear to Enjoy it ask your Paper [Papa] to let you

come for a Day or two — we have a house perched on a hil overlookking the sea; and an old castle behind us — are you not tired of London do write and tell all about yourself &c &c remember me to Rachal and and belive yours ever

Susan

When the court of George IV was at the Pavilion in Brighton, whole families stayed in the town: in 1823 Lord and Lady Cowper brought all their children, William and Caroline Lamb stayed with the Ponsonbys and brought Susan and Augustus and the inevitable doctor.

Birthdays were celebrated, sometimes with parties for the tenants. Presents were generous. When Augustus was twenty, his mother wrote:

Brocket Hall
August the 29th
1827

My Dearest own boy . . . — how very good your Father has been about writing — Susan wishes much for a letter — she sends you the only sovereign she has got to buy you a birthday present and I 4 for the same purpose . . . [16]

From her earliest days, Susan shared with Lady Caroline a fondness for the tame and wild animals at Brocket and a love of nature which, even as a child, and certainly later, she was able to communicate in her writing. Letters between Lady Caroline, Augustus and Susan never failed to give news of all the animals and birds. Dogs were an important part of the Brocket household, as in all English country houses, and news of them mattered to Augustus and to Susan. The dog Bell was a favourite; Cloe went to a friend but not the Homer puppy; and, not forgetting birds and cats, Lady Caroline wrote to her son that 'the Pea hen has laid 2 eggs and *Bijou* this morning devoured a bird *tout entier* feathers and all.'[17]

Sad as it is that such letters, with their deliberately childish emphasis on trifles, should have had to be written to a grown young man, they show Caroline Lamb to have understood the kind of things that fascinate children and to have taken the trouble to write (or dictate) them. It is a pity that she never used her undoubted talent to write stories for children, though to watch her rapid sketching must have held them entranced. The letters were

Brocket Hall July 19th 1827

My Dear Augustus

I hope you are better pray write to me and tell me how you like the place Brocket is looking beau- -tiful and all the flowers are in bloom. Lady Caroline sends her love and Dr Goddard the same, —— pray tell me who you bore your passage over is Planix park very big. all the People at Brocket send their duty to you and Little Mary at the stable that you were so fond of Mr Hewitson as well as Mr and Mrs Peacock and Mr Hyhard send their duty to you and hope you are quite well we dined at Mr Chester's yesterday Lord Boxborough

A letter from Susan (at Brocket) to Augustus Lamb. The text of this letter is included in this chapter (Panshanger MSS).

47

is coming down here next week   if you want
any book Name it   and Lady Caroline will send it you

                                        yours ever
                                              Susan

P.S.
        Susan wishes you to answer her letter

Mr Aug. Lamb

Continuation of letter from Susan to Augustus Lamb, shown on the previous page. The text is included in this chapter (Panshanger MSS).

My Dear Augustus

you never answered my letter; I will write you this one more in hopes of hearing from you — Do tell me how you employ your time and how you like your life in Phœnix park — is it as pretty as Brocket? the water has been cleaned out, & now looks beautiful, Lady Caroline often goes upon it in the boat, we also have many amusements among which shooting at a target I am most fond of — I stand at 30 yd Dr goddard at 60 or 70 yesterday I got 93 in one hour, I have once or twice beaten Dr goddard,— pray let me know how Mr Lamb is.— I am ever yours sincerely

Susan

Another letter from Susan (at Brocket) to Augustus Lamb, the text of which is included in this chapter (Panshanger MSS).

meant to be, and were, shared by Susan, who in her turn described to Augustus, now far away with his father — appointed Secretary for Ireland — in Phoenix Park, Dublin, the important events at Brocket:

Brocket Hall July 19th 1827

My dear Augustus

I hope you are better pray write to me and tell me how you like the place Brockett is looking beautiful and all the flowers are in bloom. Lady Caroline sends her love and Dr Goddard the same, — pray tell me who [sic] you bore your passage over is Phoenix Park very big all the People at Brocket send there duty to you and little Mary at the stable that you were so fond of Mrs Westwood as well as Mr and Mrs Peacock and Mr Hagard send their duty to you and hope you are quite well we dined at Mr Chester's yesterday Lord Bessborough is coming down here next week if you want any book Name it and Lady Caroline will send you it

yours ever

Susan

PS [in an adult hand] Susan wishes you to answer her letter.

My dear Augustus

You never answer'd my letter, I will write you this one more in hopes of hearing from you — do tell me how you employ your time and how you like your life in Phoenix park — is it as pretty as Brocket? The water has been cleaned out, & now looks beautiful, Lady Caroline often goes upon it in the boat, we also have many amusements among which shooting at a target I am most fond of. I stand at 30 yards, Dr Goddard at 60 or 70 yesterday I got 93 in one hour. I have once or twice beaten Dr Goddard . . .

Caroline in her letter adds to the news:

Susan says there is a great spirit risen up for shooting with bows & arrows in the County, & there will be archery meetings very soon . . . Will you tell your Father that I thank him much for his nice little note . . . it made me quite happy as I heard you were behaving very dutifully and very well — do say to him that there are no politics talk [sic] of in the county & every body here is quite quiet — the Duke of Wellington dined at Hatfield . . . , and looked uncommonly well — the partridges run rather small & thin this year . . . [18]

As the life of Susan's second protectress drew to its close, so the carefree years at Brocket were also soon to end. For Caroline Lamb, those years had held some of her greatest unhappiness. When Brocket became Susan's home and the Lambs took her into their care, the tumult of Caroline's affair with Byron was already eight years in the past. The obsessive, excited talking of which Dr Lee wrote; a predisposition to the 'high form of insanity' diagnosed by Dr Goddard but which seems to have been a form of (untreated, of course) manic-depression; the excessive drinking; the publication of *Ada Reis*, the later of her two best known novels; Byron's death; and above all, the heartbreak and trauma of the preliminaries to a separation from her husband — all this went on while the children at Brocket were playing and being educated and their various interests fostered. No one enquired — how could they at that period? — how far her physical health, perhaps an over active thyroid, bore on her psychological state. Yet the year before she died Dr Goddard was already warning her husband about symptoms of the dropsy which was such a marked feature of her last days.

Some of her behaviour — dressing up, going out alone in disguise, not caring for the conventions — was repeated, quite unconsciously, by Susan when she was in Geneva, and in those circumstances might have led to disaster. But most of it was harmless. An earlier instance recounted by Harriet Cavendish is surely no more than a sign of Caroline's pride as a young mother in her small son Augustus: '[She] rides out upon the high road, the Horse or Ass . . . led by the page in full dress, the baby on her lap and her maid and the nurses following on foot, and then wonders why the Turnpike men laugh at her.'[19]

Her drinking had been publicly known since the courtesan Harriette Wilson retailed the gossip of a maid who had been in Caroline's service. Caroline was well aware that her self-control had slipped; in an undated letter, which is clearly intended as a self-absolving confession, probably written to Dr Goddard, she reveals why:

Sir being unhappy today, I have drunk 1 whole bottle of wine which I bought for myself all at once without [food?] . . . & I did it upon hearing Mr Lamb wished to speak to me . . .

On another scrap of paper she listed the exact quantities of alcohol and laudanum which she had consumed in one day.[20]

Because of an unsuspected dark side of William Lamb's character that has recently become known — his fascination with whipping — it is now less easy to dismiss as her own mad wildness some of the phrases she used in telling her mother-in-law of the early years of the marriage: of her innocence and of William instructing her in 'things I need never have heard'.[21]

Posterity has focussed on two images of Caroline Lamb. On the one hand there is that given by her sister-in-law Emily Cowper, a very able woman, but hard and insensitive when it came to understanding Caroline's character — 'mad as Bedlam' was all she could see.[22] Caroline's favourite cousin the sixth Duke of Devonshire, who as Lord Hartington had grown up with her, her 'Dear Hart' as she always called him, had harsh things to say about her treatment by the Lambs and Cowpers, whom he frankly disliked. At Panshanger, the Cowpers' house, he noted when he was staying there in 1824 that:

Its dull here with these indifferent damn your eyes people. F[rederick] Lamb is odious, Ly Cowper absent when not excited . . .

The next day:

I rode late to Brocket, found poor Caro there in a state of sad degradation. She might have been saved had she not got into the hands of these blackguards.[23]

The other picture of Caroline Lamb is that which has emerged from her affair with Byron. Byron's friends were very articulate in their attacks (Hobhouse's 'Lady Caroline is come to town and is in mischievous activity'[24] is one of the mildest) and Byron's more partisan biographers have attributed a diabolical maliciousness and deviousness to all Caroline's actions and writings during that feverish — but in fact very short — episode and especially in the period after his death. A more balanced view[25] has suggested that it was Byron, rather than her husband, who first aroused her sexuality, and that in the literal sense passion drove her mad. For a time she behaved insanely, and later in the neurotic manner of a highly strung, talented woman with little outlet for her talents, a marriage that had turned to disappointment, and a great but frustrated potential for being a caring, loving mother. Her deep

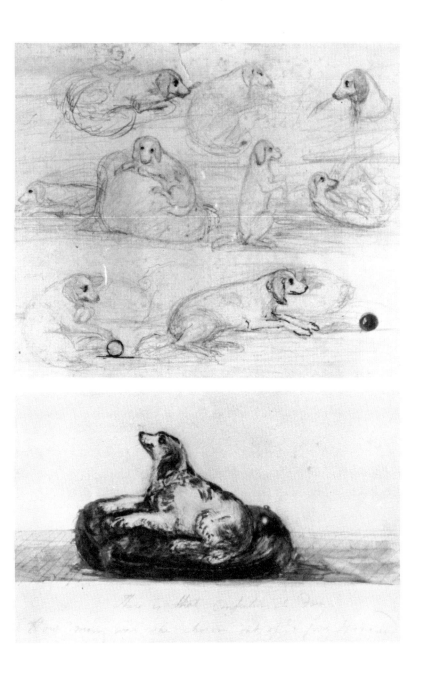

Drawings of the dogs at Brocket attributed to Caroline Lamb (Panshanger MSS).

53

A sheet of drawings by Caroline Lamb from the Panshanger MSS.

love for William remained throughout her life. Her most understanding biographer quotes the moving poem she wrote to him near the end:

> Loved one, no tear is in my eye,
> Though pangs my bosom thrill,
> For I have learned when others sigh
> To suffer and be still.
> Passion and Pride and Flattery strove,
> They made a wreck of me,
> But O, I never ceased to love,
> I never loved but thee. . . . [26]

The aftermath of these storms and the later deterioration would not have touched Susan. Her world was Brocket, and her security was given to her by this woman who treated the child as her own daughter and who indeed made efforts to order her households as would any mother and mistress of a large establishment. Here are some of Lady Caroline's shopping lists and jottings:

Seidlitz powders
Robinsons patent barley & Groats for children —
to enquire for my letters in St James Square —
6 lemons —
Tom Crofts old a new Hat
20£ to pay my bills if Mrs Crosby will be kind enough to send for them
a box of wax lights

*   *   *

The Morning Post newspaper every day
a Barell of oysters

*   *   *

provisions for the 2 Houses

*   *   *

ask Mr. Russell's Coachman to come down with with [sic] the Ponies or the one Horse [27]

All this was very expensive, as William Lamb discovered, to his dismay and surprise, when he made himself responsible for the management of the establishment during their separation.

Towards the end, Caroline returned to Brocket, where Susan was her constant companion, for the last quieter — and brave — years of her life, to sit under the trees listening to the birds; to drift on the lake in a boat, as Susan told; to enjoy music which perhaps recalled younger days when John Spencer, Susan's great-uncle, had composed music for reels on the pianoforte and 'The Honble Mr. Lamb's Delight' was a popular dance.[28]

> Where'er I go, God bless you all,
> And thus I leave thee, Brocket Hall.[29]

*   *   *   *   *

SOME HAVE WONDERED whether, if William Lamb had had a daughter of his own, his relations with the four principal women in his life — his wife, Lady Brandon, Mrs Norton, and Queen Victoria — would have been different; and especially whether his complex relation to the young Queen, a kind of father-teacher to daughter-pupil dialogue, would have reached the degree of mutual affection that for a short time it did. His latest biographer has thought that 'the mysterious child' Susan might perhaps have provided some compensation for the lack of a daughter.[30] Melbourne was fond of Susan and he fulfilled his responsibility to her up to her marriage as any father would. But there is an air of detachment about his attitude to her at this period which suggests that, since she was a Spencer responsibility and it was the Spencer side of his wife's family who had taken her in, he accepted her upbringing as his unquestioned duty but his heart had not been touched as it might have been by a Lamb relation.

By the time Susan was born, Augustus' father was already bruised by the realisation and difficult acceptance of the boy's condition. He gave few outward signs of ever accepting it. From Brooks's, as late as 1825, he wrote his son so severe a letter that Caroline had to explain that it had caused the boy 'such violent grief that it gave him 3 fits'. And yet at the beginning of that year, Augustus is instructed in such little boy details as 'Pray do not omit to clean your teeth both night and morning.'[31]

Lamb would have advocated the same kind if not the same degree of education for a girl as the careful one he had originally planned with such hope for his son. He had enjoyed and admired his wife's cultivated intelligence and free-ranging mind. Susan's education was never neglected. Her spelling was good; her early letters and her journal are well written, though the vividness and descriptive powers, and the humour, were inborn. Miss Monk, whose school Susan was attending in the last months of Lady Caroline's life, had given her lessons in writing and dancing, and had had to acquire a spelling book, Murray's Grammar, Ouiseau's Geography, as well as a sampler and silk.

These books confirm that the Lambs saw to it that Susan received an excellent education, and an up-to-date one. J. Ouiseau's *Practical Geography* was just about to go into its ninth and enlarged edition; and the famous Lindley Murray's *English Grammar*, which he had originally produced at the request of a Quaker school for girls who complained of a lack of textbooks, eventually achieved fifty editions. Susan was given one of the best educations available to girls of her period while she was at Brocket; later, when she was at school in Lausanne, comments on the lower standards of those who taught her, indirectly reveal that William Lamb did advocate a high scholastic grounding in the education of girls, though naturally, for the time, without the extensive classical content of boys' education.

Knowledge of Melbourne's preoccupation with whipping has come as a shock to many people who thought they knew the noisy, kind, lazy, tolerant, intelligent and essentially civilised man whose country was blessed with such a Prime Minister to guide Victoria's first steps in the monarchy. The only reason for considering the matter here at all is to see whether it affected Susan. She is the only girl for whom Melbourne stood *in loco parentis*, and if anyone risked being harmed by a perversion of this kind it was Susan. Two strands must be distinguished in Lamb's attitude. One is a sexual obsession with flagellation which becomes increasingly marked in his correspondence with Lady Brandon. It was probably also largely an obsession of the imagination: a man who indulged his fancy to any extent would have had less need to write about it as constantly as Melbourne did. There is something pathetic about the Home Secretary, at fifty-two, a widower, finding time to copy pages of Brantôme's *Les Dames Galantes* — a well-known sixteenth century work minutely detailing scandalous anecdotes and sexual practices — to send to his mistress in Dublin. On the other hand Melbourne differed little in this respect from his contemporaries; *Les Dames Galantes* appears to have exerted a magnetic attraction on gentlemen who came across it on bookshelves.

The other strand is in his dealings with children; and it is different. There is no evidence that, where he had responsibility for chastising a child, he allowed himself to indulge his obsession. He had as a boy been shocked by floggings at school. Though, in this complex character, a subtle difference appears between his actual infliction of a beating on Susan, and his recommendation for, and slight imaginative dwelling on, one for Lilly, Lady Brandon's daughter, or his enthusiasm for acquiring copies of Devéria's pictures of a woman spanking a small child.[32] Susan's letters, written much later when, she says, she was practising his precepts by whipping her own children, imply that the question had become a good joke between them. She remembered several such 'executions' at Brocket when she was a small child. Melbourne too remembered that he had 'sometimes chastised' her, though he also said that he 'never whipped [her] but the once for disobedience and she never disobeyed me any more.' When she was about twelve, Melbourne asked her whether she was ever whipped at school; she replied that she would never submit to such a thing. This shocked her guardian; but characteristically he felt that he could not take the trouble to move her to another school where she would be under proper discipline; and, after all, he concluded, perhaps the age of twelve was a little late for physical punishment, 'except in very extreme cases'.[33]

Melbourne knew Lady Brandon's daughter well; she was 'Lilly' to the family. His injunction to 'ask her, if she does not herself think it [a whipping] would do her good'[34] might be interpreted as gratifying himself with the titillating thought. But in the light of Susan's later letters and of the relationship which Melbourne had with Lady Brandon's Irish connections, the remark savours more of teasing, joking conversations between a child and a man she trusted. The thing must not be seen out of context. In the long correspondence between Melbourne and Lady Brandon, much of it deals with Lilly's welfare and how best to ensure that she is not taken from her mother.

When Caroline Lamb died, in January 1828, Susan was nearly ten. However fond she was of Mr Lamb, and she was, he was a remote figure and in any case had been living in Ireland for what must have seemed a long time to the little girl. At that age a sense of desolation and abandonment can be overwhelming. She was put into mourning and her physical care was undertaken by Mrs Peterson. She never in later life wrote about this time; but an odd little passage written in her journal in 1835 when she was in

Switzerland shows the marks of early sorrow and the innate tough courage which developed through grief and loneliness. On that occasion, she had been the object of a pious lecture:

to prepare me for the pains of this life. I cannot help comparing people who always teaze and torment one in the kind view of preparing one for the real torments of life, to the guardian of a man condemned to be beheaded, who would take a knife and make little incisions in the condemned one's neck with the kind intention of accustoming and preparing him for the cruel reality. The victim would say Leave me in peace and when the critical moment arrives you will see that without the aid of your preparation I shall walk with a firm and tranquil step to the fatal spot. So it is with me . . . and with the help of God I am convinced I shall meet all my misfortunes without flinching.

The strange outburst, some years after Caroline's death, reveals all too clearly the chill of the child's isolation at that time. With no Lady Bessborough and no Lady Caroline, her own parents unknown to her, her Spencer grandparents even farther away, much kindly-meant but destructive talk must have impressed on her that she faced a 'cruel reality'.

The immediate reality was William Lamb's decision to send her to boarding school. There was no other course of action possible in the circumstances. Lord Melbourne (he had just inherited the title), faced with his son Augustus and with this 'orphan' girl, acted responsibly and honourably. And he kept in affectionate touch with her. But by 1831 he was worried about Susan's future and about the expense of her education. This last point may indicate the development of what later became an obsessive though as it happened unnecessary worry over money. He consulted Mrs Norton about Susan's schooling and grumbled at what the child was costing him. Mrs Peterson was urging him to come to a decision about the future. All this he poured out to Caroline Norton, in the early days of their friendship.

Mrs Norton knew that Susan's surname was Churchill, and she suggested to Melbourne that it be changed so that the girl as she grew to adulthood would be less easily identified. Susan, in contrast to all the earlier Devonshire House 'children of the mist', was given her father's name. To call boys by their patronymic would, clearly, have led to confusing problems of inheritance; the true identity of girls however was also hidden under such names as Courtney, Stewart, St Jules or Williams. There was certainly a good deal of family discussion about this, and it is characteristic of the warm-hearted liberality of Georgiana Duchess of Devonshire that she tried to have the name of Cavendish — the Devonshire family name — bestowed on Charlotte Williams, her husband's daughter by Miss Charlotte Spencer. It remains an unexplained mystery of Susan's life, in which such trouble was taken to conceal her very existence, that she bore her father's name and that people in society, like Mrs Norton, realised at least her family's, even if not any individual's, identity.

Mrs Norton could scarcely have known the whole story, which had led, she said, to Lord Melbourne's being 'weary of this self-imposed burden of a little girl who must be fed, clothed, & grow into a woman', else she would not have reproached him with having 'weakly allowed her to be domesticated as *a plaything* in your house, you consulted your own caprice or that of Lady Caroline, and not the good of the child'. This was hard on Melbourne; nonetheless Mrs Norton felt justified in rallying him to persevere with Susan's upbringing: he had told her of the death of Dr Goddard, with the consequent lapse of a pension, and this should make it easier for him, she said, to meet the expense of the 'little castaway'.

Mrs Norton gave a good deal of thought to the matter of Susan's education for a future livelihood. The only way in which the girl, brought up as a gentlewoman, could earn her living was as a governess: Melbourne had explained that Susan ' "was accustomed to have everything the same as Caroline and to go out with her in the carriage" '. She could be educated to become a governess by going to a school — Mrs Norton knew of one such — where she would already earn part of her schooling as a pupil-teacher. Caroline Norton jokingly offered, should she herself ever have a daughter, to provide in this way 'a future subject for Miss Churchill's educating powers'.[35]

As it turned out, Susan was saved from the fate of so many unmarried gentlewomen, and did not have to become a governess in Mrs Norton's household, interesting though that would have been when Caroline Norton pioneered the fight for a divorced or separated mother's right to the legal custody of her children. Caroline Norton, through her love of her children and her suffering when they were taken from her by her husband, became a social reformer. Later, in the middle of the century, her work and her writings contributed to important changes in a variety of laws concerning the marital and wage-earning position of women.

Meanwhile, Lord Melbourne, who could so easily have avoided any further personal involvement in Susan's life at this juncture, when she could have been boarded with a family, to become a governess when her schooling was over, continued to carry full responsibility for the girl and, when she was fourteen and a half years old, arranged for her to go and complete her education in Geneva. For someone born into early nineteenth century high society but who would never be completely accepted as such, this was probably the best solution. To send such a child abroad was also the traditional solution: two of the former Duke of Devonshire's illegitimate daughters had been sent to Paris and indeed caused some concern to the English Ambassador by being there during the wild revolutionary scenes of 1789.

All the poignancy of Susan's position lies in Mrs Norton's two words: 'castaway' and 'governess'. To all appearances, she had been cast away by her father and mother, and by her mother's parents, William and Susan Spencer. Whatever family agreement may have been reached to prevent the child from being an encumbrance to her father's family, or an obstacle to her mother's Westerholt marriage, she became by this fact a castaway. But Lady Bessborough rescued her, and was succeeded by her daughter Caroline Lamb and she in turn by William Lamb. They kept faith with any undertaking that may have been given in 1818.

Lady Bessborough, with her compassionate insight into the plight of unmarried mothers, and of their daughters, so often doomed to be governesses in the great houses, and doubtless with her own feelings of anxious guilt about her children by Lord Granville Leveson Gower, would have well understood Susan's position on the verge of adulthood in 1832. She had once written about her sister Georgiana's daughter, Eliza Courtney, who however had had the privilege of being brought up by her own grandparents:

Eliza is a fine girl, and will, I think, be handsome; but tho' they are kind to her, it goes to my heart to see her — she is so evidently thrown into the background, and has such a look of mortification about her that it is not pleasant, yet *he* [her father, Charles Grey] seems very fond of her. Ld B. has this moment ask'd me whether she is not the Governess.[36]

Susan was sent abroad to finish her education. And in Geneva, the woman to whom, after his wife, Melbourne had been most attracted, and of whom Mrs Norton was retrospectively so jealous, Lady Brandon, was now to enter Susan's life.

Although she never took the place of the daughter William Lamb might have loved, he had a genuine affection for her, and he made the wisest decisions he could for her future. For her part, she always remained, as she expressed it in ending her letters to him, his 'most affectionately attached, Susan'.

NOTES

1. Panshanger MSS (Hertfordshire Record Office), Box 17, 26 August, 1841.

2. *The Miniature Magazine,* Vol. I, July 1818. *The Green Man or Periodical Expositor,* Vol. 3, 1819.

3. *The Journal of Mrs Arbuthnot,* edited by Francis Bamford and the Duke of Wellington.

4. Lord Granville Leveson Gower, *Private Correspondence 1781 to 1821,* edited by Castalia Countess Granville.

5. *Hary-o. The Letters of Lady Harriet Cavendish, 1796-1809,* edited by Sir George Leveson Gower.

6. *Recollections of a Long Life,* Lord Broughton.

7. *Hary-o.*

8. *Extracts from the Diary of the late Dr Robert Lee, FRS,* (1821-1822).

9. *Lady Bessborough and her Family Circle,* edited by The Earl of Bessborough and A. Aspinall.

10. Elizabeth Jenkins, *Lady Caroline Lamb* and *Lady Morgan's Memoirs: Autobiography, Diaries and Correspondence.*

11. Panshanger MSS, Box 18, Caroline Lamb to Mrs Crosby [undated].

12. *Hary-o.*

13. Panshanger MSS, Box 17, Susan to Augustus, 26 January 1827.

14. ibid., Caroline Lamb to her son Augustus [undated].

15. ibid., Caroline Lamb to Augustus, and Susan to Augustus Lamb. [undated].

16, 17. ibid., Caroline Lamb to Augustus, 29 August, 1827.

18. ibid., Susan to Augustus Lamb, and Caroline Lamb to Augustus, 19 July 1827 and 18 September 1827.

19. *Hary-o.*

20. Panshanger MSS, Box 18 [undated].
21. *In Whig Society, 1775-1818,* Mabell, Countess of Airlie.
22. Panshanger MSS, Box 17, Lady Cowper to her brother Frederick Lamb [undated].
23. Devonshire MSS, Chatsworth, 6th Duke's Group, 767.448, 1824, 33-36.
24. Lord Broughton, op. cit.
25. *The Byron Women,* Margot Strickland.
26. Quoted by Elizabeth Jenkins, *Lady Caroline Lamb.*
27. Panshanger MSS, Box 18, November 1825.
28. ibid., Box 13, Lady Caroline Lamb's music book.
29. Quoted by Elizabeth Jenkins, op. cit.
30. *Melbourne,* Philip Ziegler.
31. Panshanger MSS, Box 17, William Lamb to Augustus [1825].
32. Achille and Eugène Devéria were two artists much in fashion in Paris in the first half of the 19th century.
33. Panshanger MSS, Box 18, Lord Melbourne to Lady Brandon, 28 January 1831.
34. ibid., 28 February 1828.
35. Panhanger MSS, Box 37, Mrs Caroline Norton to Lord Melbourne, 7 August 1831.
36. Lord Granville Leveson Gower, op. cit.

CHAPTER THREE

Geneva

> After having been shut up in a box called the Dover
> coach, we arrived at Dover, having dined at Canterbury.
> From Canterbury to Dover I went outside the coach for
> I could bear it no longer.
>
> *from Susan's Journal*

IN 1832, GENEVA was nearing the end of its twenty-
five years of happiness, as the period between the fall of Napoleon
and the era of European revolutions came to be called. The proud,
independent republic, that had freed itself from the domination of
the Dukes of Savoy and become the stronghold of the reformed
religion in Europe, then fallen for a short time into Napoleon's
Empire, had joined the Swiss Confederation in 1815 and enjoyed,
in spite of the adjustments that had to be made on becoming one
among other equal cantons, a remarkable renaissance in its
economic, social and cultural life. Historians look back on that
'luminous' and happy period as unique in Geneva's history, when
the ancient city, still keeping many of its past characteristics of
stern virtue and an inward-looking strength, was opening out,
physically and spiritually, intellectually and artistically, to a new
phase of scientific knowledge and literary excellence, as well as to a
new grace and lightness.

The town itself was expanding: the shore opposite the old city
on its hill was made into a quay and linked to the town by a new
bridge, and the splendid Hotel des Bergues was built. Visitors
poured into the town and its surrounding *campagne*. Chief among
these were the English. The French were not popular: in spite of a
common language and the essentially French culture of Geneva,
Napoleon's wars were still too recent a memory. On her journey
through France, a curious little incident made Susan aware of

these national tensions. The party had got out of the coach to walk as they neared the Jura mountains, when:

an impudent little French boy who kept pigs hallowed out 'Loups-o, loups-o' [wolves-o] to frighten us . . . he took up great pieces of stone and threw [them] at us . . . all because he said we were Swiss although I told him we were English. Just like the French![1]

The many libraries and *cabinets de lecture* were used as clubs, especially by the English who, after the Genevese, had the distinction of holding the highest number of readers' cards. The great periodical *La Bibliothèque Britannique*, later *La Bibliothèque Universelle*, had been famous for the fearlessness of its resistance to Napoleon, and was the first to promote the local fame of Byron and Walter Scott, and of the English educational theories of Bell and Lancaster.

So welcome was the English aristocracy in Geneva society, and so cosmopolitan was the city itself, that social gatherings became the subject of satirical articles. An account of an imaginary reception listed the guests as Milady Worston and four daughters, a Russian princess, and two beautiful young Cossacks. Susan's reporting of similar events which she was to attend show little difference between satire and actuality.

Geneva society wanted music. For the first time in its Calvinist history, the Cathedral was used for public concerts. Staunch Protestants refused to accept the 'highly improper Catholic term "a spiritual concert"' and thought that it was scandalous.[2] Susan went to a concert in the Cathedral that year, and was much struck by the contrasting white dresses and veils of the ladies of the choir with the black suits of the gentlemen. The following year, the twentieth anniversary of the liberation, was celebrated by all kinds of events, including a concert in the same place about which nobody complained. When the young Liszt gave a concert in the town, everybody agreed that they were hearing the world's leading pianist.

Fashions in dress were colourful. Little evening hats, and cloaks tied with ribbons of shot-green or tartan taffeta were popular. Men wore silk tartan cravats and Englishmen were recognisable by their white serge coats and their beaver caps.

Two of Susan's relations had been in Geneva before her. Francis Almeric Spencer, Baron Churchill of Whichwood, was her great uncle. Under the name of F. Spencer of Liverpool, he had written an open 'Letter to the Genevese', a very serious essay in which he takes upon himself to advise them on various agricultural and sanitation matters, and especially to encourage them to save. Thus, he concludes, children will be fired with enthusiasm for saving, and family life and happiness and prosperity will all be enhanced.[3]

The other visitor, ten years before her arrival, had been one of her uncles, her mother's brother, said to be 'beau comme l'amour, but too sensible of it'[4] — echoing something of William Spencer's conceit.

The generation just reaching adulthood had not known war and danger; to these contemporaries of Susan, resistance to Napoleon and the joyful burst of freedom in 1815 were nothing but old tales. Well dressed and prosperous, these young people affected a bored and languid manner, and they were, in the eyes of those who had known the earlier happy years, too conventional. Even for Geneva as a whole, the fire had dimmed, freedom was a commonplace, and the first liberation from the Calvinist straight-jacket had lost its excitement. The typical Genevese, they said, in 1832 was 'moral, serious and sad', small-minded and passionless. But this was the mentality of the Ville-Haute, of the aristocracy in their big houses, and of the prosperous bourgeoisie. Across the Rhône, near the new quay, lay the old populous districts, and the market gardens and grazing lands, outside the city walls, like the Paquis. Here the people lived, workmen, artisans, lively and extrovert, and open to revolutionary ideas.

It was into this town of total strangers, with not one familiar face, that Susan was brought: unsure of her place in society, used to the freedom of life at Brocket, to the uninhibited manners of the Lambs, just released from the discipline of boarding school, and now removed from the only family she had ever known. An extrovert with a great love of natural beauty, but still very shy, she was to find herself in the family of a Geneva clergyman where she must finish her education.

The England she had left behind had seen the great Reform Bill of 1832 passed by Parliament just six weeks earlier, and her guardian was still Home Secretary.

At the end of July 1832, after a fortnight's coach journey of which every moment fascinated her, she arrived in Geneva. Her diary for that fortnight is a vivid record of European travel in the 1830s, with its age-old discomfort of coaches but with steam already for some years past shortening the Channel crossing. Before the diary proper, she lists the places where the party dined and spent the night; headed 'Journey from London to Geneva' these include, among others, Abbeville, Montreuil, St Denis, Melun, Sens, Dijon, Pontarlier, Orbe, Lausanne (at the Lion d'Or inn, she notes), Rolle and so to Geneva. Already she reveals something of her characteristic vitality and love of natural beauty:

July 13th 1832. Set off from London for Geneva after having been shut up in a box called the dover [sic] coach we, that is to say Mademoiselle Sterkey,[5] Mademoiselle Berteau, Miss Snow, Butin the femme de chambre myself and Mirabouc [the coachman] arrived at Dover We dined at Canterbury from Canterbury to Dover I went out side the coach for I could bear it no longer We arrived at 8 o'clock went to the Nags head Inn had tea went to Bed I had a room with such a delightful view that instead of going to bed I sat at the open window for a long time looking on the beautiful sea. Set off from Dover by the Crusade steamer at nine Such beautiful weather not at all ill slept on Deck the whole time arrived at Calais before 11 went to Roberts Hotel dined at 3 went for an immence [sic] long walk on the Ramparts to hear the Band play met a Greek an acquaintance of Miss Snow's we lost ourselves arrived at our Hotel a little after 7 had tea and an Italian man to play and sing to us went to bed early although I did not go when I went into my room I forgot that I looked over the church . . .

By July 17th, they are well into France:

17th Set off at 5 I was the first down as I am generally Mirabou gave me a nosegay as a reward I shall allways get it I think . . .
18th got up between 3 & 4 breakfasted and were off by 5 walked a good deal found a wood in which we picked wild strawberries until the carriage came up to us we got in dined at ½ 11 arrived at our resting place for the night at 8 o'clock Mademoiselle Sterkey having had a severe fall and hurt her head she wanted rest we asked Mirabou to stop one day he said of course if we chose to pay for another day that he would stop but that he would not else we thought of going to St Denis and Mademoiselle Berteau myself and Miss Snow taking a carriage and going to Paris and returning the same day to Miss Sterkey and then going on the next day but we found the Inn so bad and dirty that it was all we could do to dine there so we gave up the idea of going to Paris although we were within 2 hours journey of it which was very tiresome. (Mademoiselle Sterkey who allways thinks herself stronger than she really is is continually falling down)

Travellers' tales of dirty inns in France compare badly at this period with the conditions which were to be found in English hostelries.

We set off immediately after dinner and arrived at such an Inn the rooms were so dirty although a degree better than we had had in the morning after fasting nine hours you may suppose we were rather inclined to hunger and we did justice to an excellent tea and after having travelled 16 hours with only 1 hours rest we were rather tired so we went to bed immediately after. Some parts of the country between St Denis Paris and the next station are beautiful . . .

The ladies evidently were kept to a strict time-table by the coachman Mirabouc (which Susan sometimes spells this way) and were becoming more and more exhausted. Even Susan began to wilt.

Set off at 6 which made Mirabouc very angry indeed because we had to go 50 miles and he said we should be too late We dined at Sense [sic] went to see the cathedral and the Dauphins tomb . . . We arrived very late at Joigny I was so tired that I could not eat although as usual we had fasted nine hours we were so very tired that Mirabouc said that if we were in the carriage by 6 that would do we got up at 5 it was Sunday when I was half dressed Mademoiselle Berteau came to say that Mademoiselle Sterkey had had another fall and that her head hurt her so and she was so sick that we could not go till 12 at least and she advised me to go to bed again I laid down and wrote to Mrs Hunter went to see the churches after breakfast they were all full . . .

Already Susan is stimulated at the sight of her first mountain.

I climbed up to the top of a mountain the 1st we had found it was so dreadfully windy that I could hardly stand, Miss Snow came half way up but was obliged to slip down again as well as she could I got up and down quite safe put the letters for Emma in the post Dined at the table d'Hote went out shopping at Dijon stopt out very late Mademoiselle Sterkey was very cross and would not have any tea . . .
Next day we got up at 3 o'clock we slept at Salin at the foot of the 1st Jura mountain the night before Mademoiselle B—— Miss Snow and myself went to see the Salin waters Made-B—— did not dare go down for fear of an explosion or something of the sort I suppose there was a dreadful rushing of waters and while we were there something was out of order which was dangerous but it was soon put right again.
The next morning by getting up at 3 and with six horses we got up the mountain we walked the whole time . . .

The last of her three women travelling companions left her when they arrived in Geneva, and 'I went to Miss Ferrier's the same day.'

There is some reason to believe that there was an English branch of the Ferrière family. A Louis Henry Ferrière was a Clerk in the War Office: such a position implied patronage; but it is idle to speculate about whether in some roundabout way Monsieur le Pasteur Ferrière in Geneva was recommended to Lord Melbourne by a relation in London. Susan's guardian is more likely to have heard of him from the usual advertisements issued by schoolmaster pastors. The Ponsonbys quite often stayed in Geneva and could well have acted as intermediaries.

The Ferrières' house was on a high terrace, Saint-Antoine, at the edge of the old town, looking towards the Lake of Geneva and the countryside of what had been Byron's Villa Diodati.

Geneva was proud of its private schools, where boys and girls, particularly foreigners, received a good grounding in the French language as well as a sound general education. The best known and the most well established of these schools were those run by the families of ministers. These were not impoverished clergy who tutored and boarded foreign students in order to make a living — on the contrary, the Calvinist *pasteurs* of Geneva ranked high in the social hierarchy, along with magistrates and university professors. The Venerable Company of Pastors commanded great respect. The boys and girls in their care belonged to all the reformed Churches, but these were far outnumbered by the Anglicans. The education of girls was taken very seriously in Geneva, in marked contrast, at least in the case of Susan, to similar schools in Lausanne. This equality with boys in the educational field gave to the young women of Geneva a poise and freedom and dignity all their own. To the amazement of the French, a girl could walk alone in the streets and go to her lessons unaccompanied.

While she was with Monsieur and Mademoiselle Ferrière, the highlights of Susan's life were expeditions into the mountains and the countryside. These are the events which she records in her journal and quite unconsciously gives us a picture of the eager, open, courageous girl she was at fifteen.

August 9th 1833 — Geneva. Went with Miss Ferriere, Pauline Appia, Pauline Galatin, and Elizabeth de Betens to the mountain near Geneva, called Saléve. We went up the pas de l'echelle it was near ten o'clock when we were at the most dangerous part, it was almost pitch dark the moon being hid by the clouds, we had brought no lamp. Miss Ferriere was in a great fright I was quite delighted as I generally am when there is any thing in the shape of danger it is so *rare*. We arrived safe and sound at Moutier where we made a *frugal repast* and betook ourselves to rest on beds of straw made by ourselves we had brought duveys and sheets. The next morning I got up at 4 o'clock and made P.G. do the same. We took a *short* walk half way up le grand Saleve for Moutier is situated dans le creux between the petit et grand Saléve came down to breakfast.

Susan never lacked physical courage, but she also liked to show off and enjoyed frightening her school mistress:

Went to Morney visited Tarabara a hole in the mountain which goes all through, it is not very deep because it is in a projection of the mountain so that it is suspended between earth and heaven. I frightened Miss Ferriere very much by going and placing myself between the hole and the precipice there was hardly room for me to stand. Miss Ferriere says she shall never forget her feelings at the moment she shudders when she thinks of it. It was the more dangerous as the ground having no foundation might have given way it was once much more extensive and there was another great hole just over a castle but it has fallen away and the castle is now at a little distance from it. They say it crumbles away every year. We returned by a beautiful road, and crossed the pont des loups which is beautiful so picturesque just there it began to rain we were on donkeys at the douane they lent the rest of the people umbrellas I having none got wet through. Miss Ferriere P.A. and Elizabeth got off their donkies at Morney but I and P.G. went onto Moutier on ours. It did not cease raining all day, I went up into a hay loft where I slept or pretended to sleep not to be tormented with the other people at last when it was bed time that is to say when it was dark I came down not quite decided whether I would sleep there or not but the fear of thieves prevented me . . . we returned to Moutier and took a guide and began to mount le grand Saleve we preferred going by little by way paths to taking the road where the cattle go. We stopt at all the beautiful spots we found, where we read and drew at last we arrived half dead with heat and fatigue at the top . . .

Here is the girl, little more than a child, whose greatest pleasure is to be out of doors, with the animals, who had had the run of the park at Brocket, and who is already wilting at the thought of a town:

Miss F. and P.A. were so frightened at the cows. We drank some excellent cream at the 1st Chalet that we found went as far as les treize arbre [sic] so called in Patois Miss F would not go in to the Chalet because it was surround[ed] by cows on the mountains they are rather inclined to be savage particularly the Bulls to teaze Miss Ferriere or more properly speaking to amuse myself I went and spoke to the cows. The next day we returned to Geneva . . . and the forms that necessarily attend a town . . . so stupid. I felt as though I had been taken captif [sic].

Lady Brandon with her daughter Lilly[6] (whom Susan was always to call Rosa) also arrived in Geneva in 1832. She was in her early thirties. A great deal had happened to both of them since The Reverend the Lord Brandon had first suspected an affair between his wife and the Secretary for Ireland, William Lamb. The marriage had not been happy. William Lamb's sister said that Lord Brandon had been accused, by his wife's uncles, of cruelty and adultery. This clergyman of the Church of Ireland, a poet of some merit, has left a reputation for ambitious time-serving. The gossip surrounding the whole affair was so malicious that not too great credence must be attached to an anecdote, according to which he was supposed to have offered to condone his wife's relationship with William Lamb if the latter would give him one of the Irish bishoprics in the gift of the Secretary for Ireland.

Lord Brandon was determined that his wife should not have the care of Lilly, and, like Mrs Norton later in a similar involvement with Melbourne — but with less intelligence and fierceness — she fought to have custody of the girl. All through 1828 and 1829, during the legal battle which led to the *crim. con.* case against Melbourne, a struggle went on to decide whether Lilly should be the responsibility of her mother's relations, the La Touches — Lady Brandon was the daugher of Colonel David La Touche — or of General and Mrs Trevor, to whose guardianship Lord Brandon consigned the girl in his Will. Sometimes Lilly was taken abroad by the Trevors; at another period she was at school in Blackheath, London.

Lady Brandon was advised to remain incognita whenever she came to England. She used to stay in London, dangerously near Lord Melbourne, in Parliament Street, under the name of Mrs St John. Melbourne wrote to her with perfect regularity under this pseudonym, reaching her not only in London but in Paris or Nice.

Although Lord Brandon's lawsuit failed, Lilly was still kept from her mother. But in May 1832, he died, in Nice. The Trevors were not entirely happy at Mrs Trevor's appointment to be the girl's guardian; while they did not think it right 'to recommend so compleat a subversion of Lord Brandon's will as the cession of the child'[7] to her mother, they hesitated to take any action that would once again bring Lady Brandon's conduct to public notice.

71

General Trevor set out for Nice, where Lady Brandon was staying in that June of 1832, in the hope of coming to some amicable arrangement. In the event, Lilly was restored to her mother through the instrument of Sardinian law, Nice being at that time a province of the Kingdom of Sardinia. Sardinia stretched right up to the Swiss frontier: once when Hobhouse had been staying with his friend Byron, he had reached 'the Sardinian country in an hour from Diodati'.[8]

So Lord Melbourne's former mistress, to whom he was paying a pension, and her daughter, whose life appears to have been even more unsettled than Susan's, and Melbourne's ward, all meet in Geneva. They all like each other and become friends. Their first expedition took place in May 1833. Susan enjoyed it all with her usual zest. One can well imagine the endless confidences exchanged between the two insecure girls who each had found a close friend:

1833. May 12th. Went to Chamouni with Lady Brandon, and Rosa, arrived at Bonne-ville without accidents stoped there to breakfast. Rosa and I had good fun at *No. 100*. I lost my gloves, arrived at Salange we walked some part of the way we saw two most beautiful cascades, and we got some beautiful mountain flowers, we put up at the Hotel de belle vue, after dinner, which was very bad, Rosa and I walked on the Balcony which had a most beautiful view of Mont blanc, winding river, Swiss cottages, &&c. I staid there talking for a long time we then went to bed Lady Brandon would hardly let us sleep in the same room together, because she said that she was sure that we should talk instead of sleeping. We took Volpi into our room Lady B did not go to bed, she did not even lie down . . .

Then came a real mountain adventure:

Arrived at Chamouny by 6 on the road there was such a torrent and the road was so bad that it formed a sort of precipice, the carriage could not pass, and we could not either because it was too rapid for us, so the postillion an immense strong boy, pulled off his boots and carried us over, Volpi managed with great difficulty to swim across, and the carriage went to a place where the road was better and the torrent less rapid, as it was the horses could hardly do it and the carriage was rather wet. at Chamouni Rosa and I went out to take a walk we promised not to go far, but I do not know how we managed but we went to a mountain very near Mount Blanc and we kept going higher and higher until Chamouni looked quite a speck. There were no trees one side a precipice, and on the other a few brambles, sometimes our heads turned a little, particularly Rosa's, she was so frightened that I could hardly make her go on, and it was getting dark, I pretended not to be frightened although I was a little although I was more amused at last we came to a path, for we took a different one to come down, it was so small and dangerous being so slippery, that Rosa did not dare go down, so I *galloped* down a little way to give her courage, and pretended that it was very easy, at length it was getting so dark that I think that we should never have got down for we had lost ourselves, had it not been for 2 peasants who had seen us go up and had watched us the whole time, they came up and brought us each a stick with an iron point so that with their help we got down, we then dried and went to bed . . .

The next day we set off at 9 o'clock. Villiane caught a viper which we took to Geneva in spirits of wine. We slept at Bonneville because the coachman pretended that he could not go on to Geneva that night. We got a great number of mountain flowers. We arrived at Geneva without accident only that Rosa and I were not very well but the moment that Rosa saw Geneva she was quite well. I spent the day with Lady B.

The following year, in February, the fun, though unconventional, was still childlike, with two young men who now make their appearance. Henry Gage, also recently arrived in Geneva, was Irish and a member of Viscount Gage's family. He was related to Lady Brandon, whose family were not above asking Lord Melbourne to use his influence in the advancement of their young men. He was travelling for pleasure. Thomas Jeans, on the other hand, was a student in Geneva, living in lodgings. The two young men were friends and remained so in later years.

Saléve with Lady B. February 1834. Went to Saleve with Lady Brandon. She did not go up but Rosa and I Mr. Gage and Mr. Jeans we went up the little Saléve without guides I thought we never should have got up because we could not find any path. We had such fun we threw beautiful snow balls at each other. I cut my finger dreadfully against the rock, and it amused me very much to see the beautiful *red* blood on the still more beautiful *white* snow Mr. Gage put a quantity of beaver on my finger, which did not improve the looks of his hat. We made Roman punch which was very good. We got down to Morney where we found Lady Brandon on a donkey. Neither Rosa nor I had come down once but Mr. Gage undertook (against his will) to do it for us and accordingly he fell down several times. We were very glorious. There was not dinner to be had at the Inn alias Hotel, they gave us some fried eggs not half done so Mr. Gage and Mr. Jeans went to the kitchen and did them over again much to the surprise and consternation of the people.

Lady Brandon's behaviour now indirectly reveals what must have been the wildness and unconventionality of her own social life. It also raises the question whether it was these characteristics in women which attracted William Lamb.

73

At length we got off when we got near Geneva Rosa and I took it into our heads to smoke a cigar, for which the gentlemen were much obliged to us because they wished to smoke and dared not in the carriage with us, but when we did they could so we smothered Lady Brandon in smoke fortunately the carriage was open. It was not the 1st time that Rosa had smoked, but it was my first attempt, and I did it beautifully for I smoked a monstreous [sic] cigar one of the largest made, all the people stared so to see 2 young Ladies smoking it was almost dark, we went all through the town with our cigars and managed to keep them until we arrived at the Hotel if you had seen their surprise when we wished to get out of the carriage impossible we felt quite tipsy, and we could not walk we were obliged to sit upon the stairs and we were laughing so at length with the aid of Mr. Gage and Jeans we got up they went home to dress and returned to dine with us I was so ill I thought I should not be able to go in to dinner but after dressing I was better they did not come until eight o'clock, they brought Rosa and I each a packet of Ladies cigares such *neaties* parfumed [sic] . . .

What these incidents show, particularly the return to Geneva and the masquerading in the streets of the Paquis, as described in the following extract and reminiscent of the younger days of Caroline Lamb, when she too disguised herself in boys' clothes, is that Susan was still a rather wild child, but totally innocent of the impression she made and unaware of the dangers she courted. One may perhaps credit young Mr Jeans and Mr Gage with the happy fact that her mother's history was not repeated. The only social convention which weighs with Lady Brandon is that no well brought-up young lady should drive alone in a carriage with a gentleman:

Mr. Jeans went home in the carriage with me I set him down at the Calabri where there was a ball, Lady Brandon scolded him for going inside with me, it was not his fault I made him what harm would there be? —I did not get back to Miss Ferriere until past eleven and they were all very cross, more particularly so as the last time I went to Lady B's I had come back late, and with *moustaches*, and black eyebrows I had dressed myself up with a mans cloak and hat and in this dress I went all down the Paquis to waylay Mr. Gage, whom we expected after dinner it succeeded very well he came I had not courage at 1st to speak so I followed him, and when we were near the Hotel I called out *Monsieur*, he turned and I said "votre nom" upon which he said qu'est ce que cela vous fait, I said *beaucoup*, he collared (or more properly *waisted*) me turned me round so as to have the moon full in my face, and after looking at me several minutes found me out I was so frightened that I called out Mr. Gage, he said he knew it was a woman because I trembled so. Rosa then came out of the Hotel and we walked down the Paquis together to look at the lake when we came in we

Places in Geneva mentioned in Susan's journal: Mont Salève, Ile Rousseau, and Pont des Bergues. The new Hotel des Bergues is on the left in the foreground.

Geneva, Saint-Antoine where Monsieur Ferrière's school was situated. The distant countryside on the right is the region of Byron's Villa Diodati of earlier years (Bibliothèque publique et universitaire de Genève).

found a little odd looking man in the drawing room who should it be but Peligrine the Italian maid drest up, she said as she saw us dressing she had done the same to amuse us impossible for a stranger to find her out. I kept my moustaches and came back in them which called forth a scream from one person an exclamation of "quel horreur" (favorite expression among the french) from another and what was worst of all a long lecture from old Ferriere upon the impropriety of a young Lady coming home at night in that way that if an accident had happened, and besides letting my inferiors see me disfigured in that way and all such stuff as this had he know [n] what I had done, what would he [Lord Melbourne?] have said or done. Goodness or badness knows I am sure I do not — but I kept it to myself notwithstanding my wish to tell it to teaze the matter of fact old people . . .

Mademoiselle Ferrière was worried, not unnaturally, by these escapades, and especially by the close attendance of Mr Gage and Mr Jeans on her pupil:

Fort de l'ecluse. The same week we went to the Fort de l'Ecluse, and to the perte du Rhône in the Jura. Miss Ferrière let me go on condition there should be no gentlemen with us but that condition did not please me nor Rosa so I went and Mr Gage met us on the Lyons road had she known that! Lady Brandon had betted Mr Jeans no less a thing than myself that we should get back to Geneva before 12 o'clock at night, *if so*, he was to marry me she never asked my consent, Rosa and I betted a pair of Gloves I that we should be back Rosa the contrary. We had good fun and a bad dinner the perte du Rhone was very beautiful a few yards from the hole where it loses itself it forms a cascade and runs in a torrent white with foam until it approaches the gulph when as if *triste* at its approaching *apparent* end it becomes calm and loses itself in the hole from which it comes out again quite reformed a *sedate rivulet* at least so it was when I saw it in summer you cannot see it because the whole bed where we were walking is covered.

There was talk at about this time of an engagement between Lilly Crosbie (the Brandon family name) and Henry Gage. This may have been no more than a temporary romantic attachment. On the other hand, as Lady Brandon was not unduly worried at leaving them alone together, it may have been part of an ambitious plan to marry her daughter into Lord Gage's family:

Rosa and Mr. Gage had gone on a good way into a wood so to punish them Lady Brandon and I told Perrier to tell the douanier to seize upon Mr. Gage when he came up and to say he must undress and be searched the man highly amused promised we expected fine fun in seeing Mr. Gage in a passion but the man who was a bit of a coward only went up and bowing asked him where he came from, when we told Mr. Gage he was so angry. We returned and went to see another river much more curious on each side there is a monstreous wall of rock very high the bed of the river is smooth stone and just in the middle it is separated and in this separation between the 2 sides the river runs forming all sorts of odd forms . . . it is beautiful to hear the hollow musical sound it makes, in taking a good jump you might get from one side to the other but no one would try because if your foot slips you must instantly perish . . . We returned to the Inn to dinner it began to rain a little there was a very high wind and every indication of a storm we were in a little carriage so that if a very bad storm had come on we should have been in a sad plight but by degrees the moon got up and the threatened storm passed on we set off Rosa myself and Mr. Gage walked up a long hill it was so beautiful the moon was so bright when we got in we were all very stupid and sleepy I almost went to sleep once and I awoke in a great fright finding Mr. Gage and Lady Brandon staring me full in the face and laughing enough to kill themselves I was in such a passion We arrived safe at the hotel before 12 so that I won a *husband and a pair of Gloves* the latter of which I got.

This was a period when young women behaved with an artless demonstrativeness towards each other. Sisters and friends walked with their arms entwined and frequently kissed. It made no difference at all to their flirtations with young men, and Susan followed the innocent fashion:

Mr. Gage and Rosa and I went and stood at the window looking at the moon and talking Rosa and I are always kissing each other he was standing between us and as usual we kissed each other he told us a very odd story and said that if we did it again he would try and do as the man in the story that is 2 young Ladies were kissing each other and he put his head between them and received a kiss on each cheek, but Mr. G. was less successful.

Once again Susan failed to return to the Ferrières after an outing with Lady Brandon. The whole party had to sleep at the hotel because, as it was after midnight, 'the drawbridges were up'.

Lady Brandon wanted to go to bed but we were not sleepy so she put out the lamp and went to her room we galloped and Walzed all three together (new fashion) and we played at Colliana or some such name very odd amusing game in the midst of it Mr. Gage was just running round the table after me when he threw the lamp down and broke it in a thousand pieces that quieted us for a moment because it made such a crash we were afraid the people of the house would hear it and get up. At last after quarreling we said good night Rosa and I were quite angry with ourselves and we vented our anger on him it was past 4 and we felt we had done wrong to sit up alone after Lady B had retired and to have made such a noise.

Lady Brandon does not come out of this episode at all well. She no doubt was used to this kind of frolic; but Susan was inexperienced, naturally got over excited, and had enough conscience to feel some tension between enjoying the fun and keeping faith with the Ferrières. She was also missing Lord Melbourne, or at least the security of his visible guardianship.

Lady Brandon and I had a *long conversation* . . . We returned to the Hotel we dined and they dressed. I left them at the Casino and returned to Miss Ferrieres to cry (a most unusual thing) and write to Lord Melbourne theres the end of that journey.

Possibly Monsieur Ferrière wrote to Lord Melbourne suggesting that the company of Lady Brandon and her party of young people was not compatible with a proper upbringing for his ward. Whatever correspondence may have passed between them, Melbourne came to a decision, and an unhappy Susan was packed off to another school for young ladies in Lausanne. However, that belongs to the next chapter in her life. She was allowed, after a year in Lausanne, to spend a holiday in Geneva. She returned triumphantly:

20th August 1835. Set off at 3 in the morning for Geneva arrived there at 9 o'clock. Rosa was waiting for me in the carriage we went to set my servant down at her friends and from thence we went home to the campagne Sousterre belonging to Mr de Constant. Lady Brandon was very glad to see me I breakfasted in her room and then Rosa and I went with the Lady's maid to bath in the Rhône after that we dressed and went in the carriage to the cabinet litteraire Anglais.

The *campagne* where Susan stayed with Lady Brandon belonged to Charles de Constant, a cousin of Madame de Staël's better known Benjamin Constant. Charles, who had retired to a small house at Sousterre after the death of his wife, was also a writer, an observer of people and events. He had lived in China and managed a freight business, which included dealings with the London market, where he was also involved in litigation. Lord Melbourne used him as a banker to pay Lady Brandon's allowance while she was in Geneva. But he died during that same summer, in London, and Lady Brandon wrote to Melbourne in some concern about how her money was to be transferred. Melbourne also used the well-known Lafitte bank in Paris, where Lady Brandon had earlier run up bills with perfumers and dressmakers.

Lady Brandon's (and Lilly's) style had changed during Susan's absence; possibly living in the house of a distinguished Geneva family had sobered her. Susan's behaviour during the ten days of her holiday in Geneva was now that of a young lady of seventeen. Lady Brandon noticed that she was quieter and 'improved as to temper and disposition' but that her manners were not as polished as when she first arrived in Geneva from school in England. As she lost her childish tomboyishness and grew up, she also lost some of the civilised manners which Brocket and school had taught her.

The references in this part of her journal to Francis La Touche have a tinge of romantic hope which shows that he and his brother Peter were on a different footing during this short holiday from the fun-loving Henry Gage and Thomas Jeans of her first years in Geneva. Encounters were much more grown-up and ladylike than the cheerful snow-balling and cigar-smoking with the earlier friends. The La Touche family — Lady Brandon's family — had originally fled to Ireland as Huguenot refugees and had there built up a banking house which brought them wealth and fame, and ensured them a distinguished place in Dublin society. Peter and Francis La Touche could afford to travel, and Peter had arrived in Geneva only a few weeks previously from Paris.

Lady B. went out in the char and I on horseback in the evening the Mr. Latouches came . . . Got up the next day Friday at 9 o'clock it was not fine enough to bath. Went out after breakfast in the carriage as usual to the cabinet litteraire and to the Magasin des Bergues met Mr. Smith got introduced we engaged him to accompany us on horseback in the evening which he did and spent the evening with us also the Mr. Latouches . . . . in the afternoon there was to have been une fete pour les enfants and all the preparations were made but it rained so much that they were all obliged to return to town . . . We went to the English Church only Rosa & I after Church we went to Capils & Robis and eat ices then went back to dinner Francis Latouche was there. After dinner we went out in the carriage with Mr. Lacroix we saw all the preparations for the illuminations . . . we went back to town it was beautiful so perfectly well lighted up the Hotel des Bergues was splendid. We met the 2 Mr. Latouches so that we had each a Gentleman after we had made the tour of the town in the carriage we got out and walked a little on l'ile de Rousseau. We laughed very much at the loving couples we saw. The fireworks on the lake were beautiful . . . Rosa and I eat a regular supper on our return. Monday as usual we went to the English library we met Mr. Smith and asked him to come with us to the museum to see Rosa's picture as we did not dare go us two alone. In the evening we rode out with Mr.

Smith and Francis Latouche we went to Ferney . . . I rode a race with Francis Latouche.

Susan had not ridden for seven years, since she left Brocket for boarding school, at the age of ten. She wrote and told her guardian how much she was enjoying it; she was stimulated to take risks as she had been earlier on her mountain walks. Caroline Lamb had also been a dashing and fearless rider.

Manners, social skills and old affections were now all to be put to the test by the presence in Geneva of Lord Bessborough, Mr William and Lady Barbara Ponsonby and their daughter Fanny Ponsonby. William Ponsonby had been Caroline Lamb's closest brother. He seemed to understand and to be able to calm her distraught mind, with a mixture of common sense and affection which cut through gossip and malice to the truth of the person. He never lost touch with Susan who relied on him and trusted him, as she had his father Lord Bessborough in the Brocket days. They drew Susan into the English social circle for the few days left of her holiday. 'I had hardly done breakfast when Lord Bessborough called he gave me a very pretty basket and invited me to come and dine and spend the evening there . . . I accepted.' Then Lady Barbara called on her and:

I went there to dinner in the evening there was to be a soiree dansante the German band was hired. The rooms were beautifully lighted up. I made friends with Lady Rend[le]sham & her two daughters Lord & Lady Warwick Lord Brook[e] their son he is rather conceited rather handsome & only 18. Lady Caroline [Neeld][9] . . . is very amiable and pretty.

Lady Barbara Ponsonby introduced her to the Hon. Mrs Cunliffe, who, Susan was told, had known her when she was a child, though Susan did not remember her. The meeting would have revived painful memories for Mrs Cunliffe. As Emma Crewe, she had had a poem dedicated to her by William Spencer; but there had also been a rumour that Mrs William Spencer had prevented her marriage to Lord Dudley by making him believe some ill report of the young woman.

Before taking leave of the Ponsonbys — 'Lady Barbara gave me a very pretty bijou and promised to come and see me at Lausanne' — she went to see Mademoiselle Ferrière. She did so rather than attend the English church that Sunday morning. Lady Brandon put it down to her shyness with these older, staider, more respectable people. Indeed, Lady Brandon, who must have realised the ambiguity of Susan's position, was quite sharp in her judgment of the Ponsonbys' attitude to the girl. 'I wonder', she wrote to Lord Melbourne, 'as they all seem to like her so much that they dont have her to live with them, particularly in a few years when her Education will be finished instead of her going as a Governess if she is not married'.[10]

If Susan's social standing was ambiguous, Lady Brandon's was even more so. She tried to use Susan's relationship with the Ponsonbys and their circle to advance her daughter's prospects, realising that her own history made her presence unacceptable in society. Lady Barbara 'told Susan she was sorry not to know Miss Crosbie as she should like to have had *her* — I think it was *rather* impertinent entre nous as she might have called upon me the day she came to visit Susan & if she had then invited Lilly to go with Susan I should not have prevented her for I am always too happy when Lilly has any amusement. I put myself entirely out of the question a year & a half ago. There were several very vulgar English here', she adds, 'who had the impertinence to send her invitations without either calling or inviting me'.[11]

Susan's hopes of leaving Lausanne were raised by Lady Brandon in a selfish if not a cruel way. Susan was greatly excited by a visit which she and Lady Brandon paid to 'Melle Mérienne a friend of the Queen's [Queen Adelaide] she is a very nice person and if she consents Lady B. intends doing all she can to get me there with her'.

Mademoiselle Mérienne belonged to an old Geneva family, and was, as Lady Brandon said, 'a perfect gentlewoman, very sensible, cheerful & well informed, and decided at the same time. Susan would respect her and she would form her manners'. Lady Brandon was nothing if not frank with Lord Melbourne about her motives, though she admitted that she cared for Susan who was very much attached to her and a great friend of Lilly's: 'It would be of great use to Lilly, for if Susan is with Melle Mérienne, Lilly will go there very often . . . she can't bear going as she is alone, but Susan being there it would make it quite different . . . Pray dont refuse me & answer me immediately . . . '[12]

So the glorious holiday ended and Susan returned to Lausanne, 'in great woe'[13] but buoyed up with the hope of returning for Christmas and, even more, of becoming a protégée of

Mademoiselle Mérienne. If the plan succeeded, she told Lady Brandon, her happiness would be perfect, for what more could she ask for than to be with someone whom she could look upon as a friend and to be near Lady Brandon. For all her gaiety and courage, and the affection in which she was held by Lady Caroline Lamb's family, there spoke a lonely girl who was still, as she wrote to Lord Melbourne, 'frightened of new faces'.[14]

NOTES

1. *Journal.*

2. *L'Europe centrale,* 31 July 1834.

3. Lettre aux Genevois, F. Spencer de Liverpool. *Brochures genevoises, 1820-1830,* Geneva University Library, GF. 567.

4. *Emma Darwin: A Century of Family Letters,* edited by Henrietta Litchfield, Mrs Josiah Wedgwood to her sister, from Geneva, 1825.

5. This was probably a relation of the Rev. Alexander Sterky, who had been Chaplain to Princess Charlotte. He described himself to the Duke of Devonshire, whose patronage he frequently sought, as of foreign birth but as having lived most of his life in England. He had been ordained in the Church of England by the Bishop of London. After Princess Charlotte's death he found himself shunned by the Prince Regent's circle where formerly he had been in a position of trust. (6th Duke's Group, 136, 196, 274, 337, Devonshire MSS, Chatsworth.) Susan's Melle Sterk[e]y was journeying to Geneva where she seems to have lived.

6. *The Complete Peerage* states that Lord and Lady Brandon had an only son, Maurice, who died an infant in 1816. *Burke's Dormant and Extinct Peerages* (1883) mentions their daughter, Elizabeth Cecilia, who in 1837 married Henry Galgacus Redhead Yorke.

7. Panshanger MSS, Box 17, from Henry Trevor to Lord Melbourne, May 1832.

8. *Recollections of a Long Life,* Lord Broughton.

9. Lady Barbara Ponsonby's niece, and sister of the seventh Lord Shaftesbury, the famous philanthropist.

10-13. Panshanger MSS, Box 17, Lady Brandon to Lord Melbourne, 30 August and 10 September 1835.

14. Panshanger MSS, Box 17, Susan to Lord Melbourne, August 1835.

CHAPTER FOUR

Lausanne

> Lord Melbourne will not say a word about my going to
> Geneva. Tis very naughty of him.
>
> *from Susan's Journal*

WHEN SUSAN WAS first made to leave the Ferrières and
the social delights which Lady Brandon and Lilly, with Mr Gage
and Mr Jeans, had provided in Geneva, she was in no mood to look
with favour on her new teachers. In the end, it was in Lausanne
and not Geneva that the future pattern of her life was settled.
Meanwhile she had to go through the phase of adolescent love,
and of being loved for the first time. In Lausanne she finally grew
out of her Brocket childhood.

She took with her her English passport, which the State of
Geneva had returned to her when she left for Lausanne in the
neighbouring Canton of Vaud. The curious anonymity with which
Susan was so successfully cloaked throughout her youth is evident
even in such an identifying document as a passport. She certainly
had one, and both Geneva and Vaud took note of it when they
gave her a foreigner's residence permit; but she is not listed in the
Foreign Office's register of passports, where all the journeys of her
relations can be followed. A simple explanation for the absence of
her name may be, however, that in 1832 she was, at fourteen and a
half, very much a minor.[1]

She was escorted to the stage coach in Geneva by Mademoiselle
Ferrière on 22 July 1834. First impressions were bad:

I found Melle Mange and her pensionnaires they had already secured the
best places and left me one in the middle near Melle Mange the ugliest
creature ever seen fat enough to have made 3 common sized women, with
a brown wig curled all round and frightful features. At six o'clock in the

evening we arrived at Lausanne we took tea at her nieces I never was so bored in my life and they were all so triste because Francois Porter [Porta] her youngest nephew was to set off the next day for South Amerika. — Nothing particular passed for the 1st fortnight after which the Moldavian princes returned from their voyage and as they were our neighbours that enlivened me a little a pretty caracter [sic] I give of myself. I was soon introduced to them and Mr. Jean immediately commenced his cour which as he was the handsomest and most fashionable looking vexed all the girls very much. He fell in love with me and so did I *at length* with him.

In order to understand the development of the affair and the comings and goings of the characters in the play, it is necessary to explain the scene. Mademoiselle Mange's establishment was in the oldest part of Lausanne, at the heart of the steep medieval city, next to the Cathedral, in the Rue Cité Derrière. Next door was a house which for centuries had been the priest's and after the Reformation the minister's. In 1834 it was lived in by Monsieur Louis de Vallière, Secretary to the Council for Public Education. He ran a school for foreign boys, which was also a boarding house for young foreign gentlemen who were registered students at the Academy of Lausanne. The house had been used in this way for many generations: Edward Gibbon had been sent there in 1753 in an attempt to induce him to return to the reformed religion from his recent conversion to Rome. The Moldavian princes now lived there. The garden adjoined Mademoiselle Mange's. Also in the same street lived the Porta family, as Susan noted; one of them, Charles Porta, was later to play an important though still unexplained part in her religious life.

The Moldavian princes' relations with Susan in one way had all the ingredients of a Mozartian opera, but in another sense they were the means by which she grew through her first love and came out of it unscathed. She was able to look back on it with humour and with tenderness. The princes were members of the ancient Cantacuzenus family, which at one time had reigned in Byzantium. Later this royal family fled to Moldavia, in what is now Romania. For centuries power in that area had swung between the overlords of Russia, Turkey and the Greeks of Constantinople; the family's reign finally ended in 1716, though its members continued to be active and sometimes eminent in various countries. By the time that the four young Cantacuzenuses arrived in Lausanne in 1833, many of their fellow-countrymen, under French influence which had spread into Eastern Europe, were students in France and other

French-speaking countries.

Prince Jean was twenty-one when Susan first met him; Prince Basile, who became a reliable friend when his brother's passionate affair was over, was nineteen. It began with Prince Jean sending her:

some bonbons and a rose with a verse in German which ended with vergiss mein nicht. After that he asked me one evening if I would allow him to write to me having something to say which he could not tell otherwise. I told him to do it if he thought it right notwithstanding that was not quite his opinion he did it he wrote to tell me how much he loved me && I did not of course answer him and this lame correspondence continued for some time until it became regular on both sides the servants were in the secret and my maid used to give the notes to and receive them from his servant. This continued for a few months he was always in the garden and I at my window and when we were in society he used to dance with me all most the whole time and if there was no dancing he was at my side everyone remarked [on it] . . .

Then the Prince, carried away by his love, had an idea which was wonderfully characteristic of the period in which the young people lived, just as their behaviour was of their respective nationalities. Prince Jean, with his passionate oriental ancestry, threatened to behave like a Byronic or a Wertherian hero. Susan, however, describes the scene with the cool humour of a Jane Austen:

. . . no one thought that he loved me enough to have sworn that he would either *live or die for me* he asked me once to kill myself for and with him and when I refused this most *obliging offer* he taxed me with cowardice.

For a time she was really in love:

If anyone should ever read this pray do not think that I entered into this secret correspondence so easily I struggled hard at first but at length *he* and *love* were stronger and forced me to do that which my conscience and my honour forbid but this could not last long that most perfidious of all perfidious women Madame de Valiere found it all out. One evening she told Mr. Jean that she had been told and knew for sure that he and I corresponded and thus she made him own all all the same evening the société des pauvres was here I had written to tell him he might come and as I knew he wished it very much I was surprised that he did not how little did I guess the cause! Mrs. de Valiere was very singular she said j'ai une telle envie de donner un souflet morale [sic] à quelque un I said in laughing est ce alors à moi Madame qu'est dirigé ce désir obligeant her answer was vous ne savez pas peut être combien il est près de vous — donnez seulement je ne le crains pas was my answer.* Soon after she asked me who occupied the room above looking out on the garden I said it was mine she asked if she could have a moments conversation with me we left the room and when she was in mine she told me that Mr. Jean had told her *all* that he was repentent quite repentent, that he understood that it was quite a folly and such things as that. I was thunderstruck and indignant at his behaviour. I immediately told her that he had written to his Uncle about me at this moment Melle Mange came in. Mad. de V. said she intended telling all to her I conjured her to be silent and I got so agitated that she left the room in a fright when she was gone I told all to Melle Mange she was very kind but I will pass rapidly over that. The next morning I received a letter from Mad. de V. to make her excuses to me for the harsh way in which she had judged me she said she had been mistaken, and that she begged I would tell her at what hour I could receive her as she had many important things to say she further said she had *his* permission to take this step.

The Prince was serious too, and Susan's first attempts at coquetry were wasted, because Prince Jean was now quite ill.

The next evening was our musical society . . . I took the resolution not only to go but to play to show him how indifferent he was to me I chose a melancholy air called *Romance de Joconde On revient toujours à ses premiers amours*. I never once looked up until it was my turn to play so that I did not know whether he was there or not when the music had finished the dancing began. I refused every one and should not have danced at all had not Mad. de V. made me by saying she would not unless I did so to please her I danced had I known her intention I should not have done so but I thought she had retreated merely by compassion for my unhappy situation but not in the least she had told Mr. de Vos to pay his court to me the whole evening and had tried to make me dance that people might think me coquette and that she might tell Him who in the meanwhile was ill at home. He was almost delirious they thought he was going to kill himself. He was always saying Oh elle ne m'aime plus et je l'aime toujours Oh mon Dieu mon Dieu! He wrote me such a touching letter. At length what with his letter and Lisette's intreaties I was prevailed upon to give him some more of my hair and to write a few lines to assure him of my forgiveness and of continued affection. This restored him a little and in a short time we were again in full correspondence notwithstanding all the spies . . .

---

*There's someone to whom I should very much like to give a moral slap . . . Is that obliging wish directed at me, Madam? . . . Perhaps you dont know how near to you it is — Give it then I'm not afraid . . .

First love could not go on at this pitch of intensity, although Monsieur Jean had taken the matter seriously and had written to his uncle about Susan. She does not say precisely whether he was requesting permission to propose marriage to her. But by now her feelings had cooled, though she remained acutely aware of him:

At length I put a stop to our correspondance at two balls I offended him at the 1st Melle Mange had ordered me not to dance with him I told him so but he continued to plague me and he was so unhappy that every one remarked it. It was the night that I first made acquaintance with Mr. Auguste Grenier the handsomest man in Lausanne and as he payed me his court the whole evening that tormented *Him* still more. At another ball given by Madame de Vallière I danced once with him but only once . . . I really was too rude and cruel to him . . . the next day I received a most cold and yet tender letter from him I wrote him one back in return but before he got it I received one from him to beg my pardon and to say that he ought to bear every thing which came from me and that he was determined to have patience for the future whatever I might do.
Things went on in this way until about March when I thought I remarked a change in him . . . and to be sure I sent him back the locket with his hair at the same time I wrote to tell him to send back the contents of the one he liked the *best*. Instead of doing so he put himself in a passion said it was I who was changed and that he never would return me my hair nor his either for he burnt it. But he did not deign to answer me more than by sending me back a silver pencil case wrapt in a dirty piece of paper.

Monsieur Jean then became ill again, and 'Mr. Paylis the doctor who en passant is in love with me more because I am English than for my bright eyes I think, took 5 lbs of blood from him . . . '
Lady Brandon saw the affair less romantically and, quite unconscious of her own lack of supervision when the Ferrières had trusted her with Susan, reported from Geneva in a letter to:

Dearest Ld M
. . . [Susan] is allowed too much liberty, she goes into the town two or three times a week by herself & I believe has a flirtation with some Greek Prince or other who is en Pension next door to Melle Mange.[2]

Susan was in some ways very much a child still, enjoying ice creams and long gossips with the other girls. At the same time, while feeling flattered by the attentions of the men she met and while enjoying dances and concerts, she was honest with herself:

Last night there was not one gentleman de connaissance so that for the 1st time since I have been at Lausanne I had no one to flirt with. If any one reads this they will think I am very legère but really du fond du coeur I do not think I am more so than most other girls but they dare not annonce [sic] what they feel and like, and I *do* there's the only difference.

On one or other occasion, she meets all four Cantacuzenus brothers, but one Sunday 'Mr. Basile and I made friends we had never hardly spoken to each other before and today we spoke to each other as though we were intimate friends we spoke the whole time about *him* with as much ease and confidence as though he had been Rosa c'est beaucoup dire . . . '

Lady Brandon was critical of the education which Susan was getting at the Mange establishment. Her comment to Lord Melbourne implies that they had in the past discussed his views on the education of girls, and that he expected a good academic standard for them. This was one of his eighteenth century characteristics; for it was the Victorians who lowered their expectations of a girl's achievements in relation to her brothers'. Lady Brandon wrote that Susan's school work in Lausanne was ' . . . more suited for a Lady's Maid than for a Governess — Except Accomplishments, which I dont think *you* [Lord Melbourne] consider the most necessary part of a woman's Education. Her mind is totally uncultivated, she never reads . . . The principal thing Melle Mange cares about is that she should know how to mend stockings & she is forced to devote hours to that work'.[3]

Although the balls and the flirtations were all great fun, the girl was conscious of a void in her life. There was the natural reaction after the cooling of first love; but there was also a desire to be with friends with whom she could be herself; and above all she found herself longing for the familiar faces of her childhood, in spite of the shyness which she had felt when she saw them in Geneva. The shadow of a governess' life was already nearer:

Just received a letter from Rosa. Lord Melbourne will not say a word about my going to Geneva tis very naughty of him . . . Rosa tells me that Lord Bessborough & Lady Barbara are or have been at Geneva if they do not come and see me I shall be very much surprised as Mr. Ponsonby promised me to come . . . Kate . . . tells me her aunt is to arrive at Paris with Mr. and Mrs. Lees I have written by return of Post to beg them to come as far as Lausanne but I suppose they will not. It appears that Lady Emily Ponsonby[4] thinks of taking Kate as governess for her children I should think she would be happy there . . .

Prince Jean was often in her thoughts still. She wanted to give him a present, and took some trouble to order his favourite brand of cigars:

Madame de Vallière is gone to Bex for a month and the princes are gone with her . . . How lucky I no longer love *Him*. I sent him the cigars he sent to thank me and to ask me how much they cost. I sent word back that I thought it a very impertinent question and that he had spent more for me last winter in bonbons and nosegays but that if he wished it I would send him in my *bill*. Mr. Basil sent me a beautiful laurier rose which he begged I would take care of and keep *in my own room*. I am so triste so very triste. And Lord Bessborough is not come how unkind!

Two months later, when the week in Geneva was only a glowing memory, faithful William Ponsonby arrived with his daughter Fanny whom Susan had known as a child.

. . . I was at breakfast I heard a carriage come up to the door who should it be but Mr. Ponsonby, Fanny and Miss Williams . . . We went together to see the Cathedral they found it beautiful. The day before I had sent an aumonière to Lady Barbara and a purse to Fanny.

Then the winter came. Lady Brandon's fear that she might be stricken with the approaching cholera and that Lilly would be left an orphan receded. The Ponsonbys went to spend the winter in Paris. So did the La Touches. Susan buoyed herself up with the hope that soon she would return to Geneva to live with Mademoiselle Mérienne. Lord Melbourne had become Prime Minister for the second time and was unlikely to concern himself with the feelings of his ward.

*   *   *   *   *

SUDDENLY, WITH NO explanation and no hint of previous discussion or instruction, Susan writes in her journal:

December 24th, 1835, Thursday. I am to be baptized and confirmed at 12 o'clock how disagreeable.

The day before she had been subjected to two homilies from Mr Curtat, the minister who baptised her (and who had in fact been giving her some instruction), and from Mademoiselle Mange.

These well-meaning people succeeded only in bringing out the stoical and independent aspects of her character. The ceremony itself was gloomy and the whole thing embarrassing and, in a subtle way, diminished her already precarious sense of identity:

How glad I am that today is past I dreaded it. Mr. Curtat only said Susan he forgot Harriett and Elizabeth. The ceremony took place at the German Church Mr. Blattner[5] Mr. Charles Porta and Melle Mange were the only persons present.

This raises a host of questions. First in Lausanne itself, why was it thought necessary to baptise the seventeen-year-old girl? Mademoiselle Mange was related to the Swiss minister Mr Charles Porta, and the most likely explanation is that, in the course of conversation, Susan had been unable to show any evidence of having been baptised. This might well have disturbed Mademoiselle Mange. For whatever reason, Mr Porta then requested permission — presumably from Susan's guardian, Lord Melbourne — to arrange for her baptism. The Home Department of Vaud forwarded the permission, when it came, to Mr Porta, but unfortunately this document has not survived. Meanwhile Mr Antoine Curtat, minister of the Swiss reformed church in Lausanne, had been instructing Susan. But there is still no explanation as to why the ceremony was performed almost in secret, and in the German church.

It is hard to believe that, when Lady Bessborough took the baby into her care in 1818, she did not have the child baptised. Convention alone would call for baptism which, even if performed in a private house, would usually appear in the parish register. Besides, Lady Bessborough was a believer and, however much she might join in attempts to conceal Susan's birth, would not have left the child unbaptised. Moreover, Susan said that Lady Bessborough was her godmother, with all that that implies, and that she had been given three Christian names — Susan Harriett Elizabeth — which she mentions. The fact remains that, so far, no register in any of over thirty parishes where her baptism might reasonably be supposed to have taken place contains the record of Susan's christening. It is possible, in view of the close-knit circle of Lady Bessborough, Caroline Lamb and the young Duke of Devonshire, and their friendship with Harriet Spencer, that Susan was baptised privately by the Duke's chaplain, the Rev. Richard Smith, and that he did not, as legally he should have, record the baptism in the local parish register. Later, Lord Melbourne was to search for such a record; what he found is part of the story of her engagement and marriage, into which her own family's follies and tragedy are woven.

Religious instruction had not been neglected at Brocket. Caroline Lamb, like her mother, was a believing Christian and wished her son 'to read your Bible and get on sufficiently to be confirmed it will be a proper and a good thing . . .'.[6] One cannot suppose that Susan, at Brocket and in her years at boarding school, should have been unversed in at least conventional Anglican practice. And she possessed her own prayer-book, once left at Melbourne House. Beyond that, the cheerful, though perhaps only superficial, agnosticism of Melbourne doubtless set the tone. At one of Lady Holland's dinner parties, he told the company 'that he remarked to the Bishop of London that it was not easy to know whom to pray to, or what to pray for . . .'.[7] Yet he once ended a letter to Lady Brandon with the words, 'May God have you in his holy keeping . . .'[8] — surely an unusual blessing, especially in the circumstances, to write to one's mistress. His agnosticism, however, never lessened his deep interest in theology and ecclesiastical history, of which he had a wide knowledge.

Susan, at the end of 1835, was now a baptised and confirmed member of a protestant, reformed church. On Christmas Day she made her first Communion in Lausanne Cathedral, and was moved by the experience. In a few years' time religion was to make such an impact on her that, in language and style, she seemed a different person. Her later journal is written in a fervent evangelical idiom, familiar in much nineteenth century non-conformity but almost startling to find in the same volume as the jottings of the gaily courageous girl formed in Regency England. The change was brought about by Mr John Nelson Darby, one of the founders of the Plymouth Brethren sect.

All this was in the future. At the end of 1835, she was still a flirtatious girl who could 'almost wish to be ill so that some great *evenement* would happen to change a little [sic]. Oh what a very handsome man I saw yesterday with Mr. de Langallerie'.[9] She was also a young woman on the threshold of one of the most difficult years of her life, during which her family history was at last going to impinge on her and some of it to be revealed to her. She would have to call on all her resources of hope and courage.

NOTES

1. Public Record Office, Foreign Office Papers, FO 610, 612.
2, 3. Panshanger MSS, Box 17, Lady Brandon to Lord Melbourne, 10 September 1835.
4. The wife of Lord Bessborough's second son, Frederick Cavendish Ponsonby.
5. Minister of the German Church in Lausanne.
6. Panshanger MSS, Box 17, Caroline Lamb to her son Augustus [undated].
7. *Recollections of a Long Life,* Lord Broughton.
8. Panshanger MSS, Box 18, Lord Melbourne to Lady Brandon, 20 August 1829.
9. The de Langalleries (or de Langalerie) were a leading Lausanne family. The Chevalier de Langalerie of an older generation was a noted mystic in the Quietist tradition and well known to Madame de Staël.

CHAPTER FIVE

Marriage

[Mr. Basile] was frank with me and when people are so I cannot even if I wished it be otherwise.

from Susan's Journal

THE PAGES OF Susan's journal which run from January 1836 to August 1837 have been cut out, by some unknown censor, leaving stubs about an inch wide. Random words on the stubs make it clear that her prospective marriage was the subject about which she wrote, the obstacles which she encountered and at times the anguish she suffered.

Susan gives the impression of having reached this stage in her life without knowledge of her true parentage or of the circumstances of her birth. Girls in her position were often told such facts only just before marriage. Caroline St Jules, daughter of the Duke of Devonshire and Lady Elizabeth Foster, used as a child to be introduced as a French orphan, and Susan was described as an orphan in her marriage settlement. Caroline St Jules was greatly upset upon learning the truth from, it is said, George Lamb, William's younger brother, whom she was about to marry.

Susan met her future husband, Aimé Cuénod, at a masked ball given by Monsieur and Madame Perdonnet in Lausanne. Vincent Perdonnet was a Swiss who had had a successful career as a stockbroker in Paris. The Perdonnets were among the leading hosts of the town: the family in the past had entertained the Bonapartes and in the future were to receive the Prince of Wales, later King Edward VII. A ball at *Mon Repos*, in its great park, would have been a splendid occasion. It must have taken place early in 1836, for up to the cut pages of the journal there is no mention of Aimé Cuénod, and by April of that year Melbourne had already given his consent to the marriage. But things were not to run as smoothly as that for Susan.

The year 1836 could hardly have been a less propitious one in which to expect Lord Melbourne to devote time to his ward. The Prime Minister's second ministry was beset with political struggles; his relationship with William IV was at best uneasy; and he still had the care of his son Augustus, who died that November. But over everything loomed his implication in the impending Norton divorce case where once again he was cited as co-respondent. He could not conceal his anxiety that the Brandon affair was about to be repeated, and Mrs Norton noted 'the *shrinking* from me' when she went to see him at Downing Street.[1] The trial, which again resulted in his favour, took place in June. Any progress in Susan's affairs was therefore scarcely to be hoped for, slowed down as it would have been in any case by Melbourne's usual indolence and unwillingness to bestir himself over anything that did not arouse his immediate interest, though the news of a suitable marriage for Susan would undoubtedly have been welcome to him.

Aimé Timothée Cuénod was the second son of the minister of a country parish, Villette, on the shores of the Lake of Geneva, a few miles from Lausanne. The village and its ancient church back onto the steep terraced vineyards which the area owes to a twelfth century bishop of Lausanne. The Cuénods traced their ancestry in Vaud with certainty to the early sixteenth century, where they were small landowners, lawyers, burgesses and soldiers. Aimé was trained in the law, and later — though this belongs to his married life — became a banker. As a young man he was known as 'le beau Cuénod'.[2] He was ten years older than Susan, and she was still a minor. The love that sprang up so quickly between the handsome man of twenty-eight and the lively, impetuous but staunch girl was to be severely tested during the next eighteen months; it endured to the end of their lives.

Lord Melbourne's consent to the marriage was unqualified:

Downing St
April 20 — 1836 —

Having had the Care of Miss Susan Churchill from her infancy, & being her sole Protector I hereby consent to her Marriage with Monsieur Aime Cuenod

Melbourne

94

Lord Melbourne's first consent to Susan's marriage, which is quoted in full in the text (Archives cantonales vaudoises).

he wrote on a plain sheet of paper.[3] In September of that year the Department of Justice and Police of Vaud certified that there was no obstacle to the marriage, a dispensation having been granted releasing the bride from the legal obligation of having the banns published in her own native parish. The only documents that would be required by the officiating minister, said the Home Department, were Lord Melbourne's consent of 20 April 1836, and Susan's Lausanne baptismal certificate of 24 December 1835. In the event, this last document was, it seems, to prove insufficient, as it was a purely religious statement that she had been baptised, whereas a copy of a baptismal entry in an English parish register would have provided legal proof of her parentage and place of birth.

From this point onwards, and no doubt because of the mystery and uncertainty of her origins, things began to go wrong for Susan and Aimé.

In April 1837, a whole year after his first consent, Lord Melbourne was asked to produce another. It is subtly but significantly different from the first one:

> Downing St —
> April 8 — 1837

I as the Guardian & as having the charge & custody of Miss Susanna Churchill do hereby give my consent to her marriage with Mr Aime Cuenod —

> Melbourne[4]

First, there is a change of name. Never before had Susan been called *Susanna*, though admittedly the names were in general and for most people interchangeable. The second difference between the two consents is that in the first one Lord Melbourne states that he had had 'the care of Miss Susan Churchill from her infancy'; but the terminology of the second consent is much more legally precise: 'I as the Guardian & as having the charge & custody of Miss Susanna Churchill . . . '.

No doubt there were a great many matters to be clarified. The Cuénods, with their solid, respectable background, would have wanted to know in some detail the identity of this young woman living in a Lausanne *pensionnat*, with no family but in some mysterious way the ward of the English Prime Minister. Vaudois

Lord Melbourne's second consent to Susan's marriage, which is quoted in full in the text. (Archives cantonales vaudoises).

law required certain documents for a marriage: at least some proof of parentage and place of origin. It was customary in well-to-do families to have a marriage settlement confirmed by legal contract, and surely Miss Churchill would not come quite penniless to the partnership? But it was the first question, that of identity as certified by an English parish register, which was to be the stumbling block and which probably caused the delay of the marriage for over a year. The matter of identity would be closely linked with the provision of a dowry.

The story which ended happily with the marriage of Aimé and Susan in August 1837, is extremely complex. Susan herself plays no part in it, for it is about people and events in England in 1817 and 1818. How far they involved her mother, Harriet Spencer, and whether they were mainly or partly the reason why she and George Spencer-Churchill did not marry, is a matter for conjecture. In the light of events, and of the relationships of the people involved in them in 1817 and 1818, the conjectural conclusion to the argument in these pages seems a reasonable one. The main clue is a baptism entry in a London parish register.

In the baptism register of St Marylebone church in London there is the following record of a child's baptism and date of birth:

17 April 1818   Susanna Churchill

daughter of   {   Susanna Adelaide Law
                            and
                     George Spencer Churchill
                        Marquis of Blandford

                                               Born 14 March[5]

When, in 1836, Melbourne was asked for the papers required for Susan's marriage settlement, there is no doubt that he caused a search to be made in the registers of London's parishes. This entry relating to a Susanna Churchill, daughter of the Marquis of Blandford, was copied by the curate of St Marylebone on 18 April 1836, two days before Melbourne wrote his first consent to Susan's marriage. Whether he received it before or after writing his consent is doubtful, because he still, in April 1836, refers to her as *Susan*. But at some point he received the copy, and kept it among his papers.[6]

Be it known to all interested therein That I the under si[gned]
William Lord Viscount Melbourne in my capacity of sole Gua[rdian]
having the Guardianship of Miss Susanna Churchill an Orphan and a M[inor]
residing at Lausanne Give by these Presents power and authority to M[essrs]
Colonel Charles Sigismund Cerjat of Lausanne and Pierre Aimé de Pa[lezieux]
Falconnet of Vevey in the Canton of Vaud in Switzerland to represent me [in a]
Marriage Contract about to be made between the said Miss Susanna Chu[rchill]
with Monsieur Aimé Timothée Cuenod Son of Monsieur The Reverend [Mr]
Samuel Cuenod Minister at Villette near Lausanne to authorize the said Con[tract]
and to have it stipulated and settled by Divine Assistance –

First – That Miss Susanna Churchill becomes the Wife of the said
  Husband with all her property present and future Subject to the tru[st of]
  a Settlement made in her favour of the sum of Three thousand t[hree]
  hundred and one pounds four shillings and nine pence Three pounds [per]
  centum consolidated bank annuities transferred in the Books of the [Bank]
  of England in the names of the said Charles Sigismund Cerjat a[nd]
  Pierre Aimé de Palezieux Falconnet.

Second That her present property consists

  A Of the said sum of Three thousand three hundred and one pounds four s[hillings]
    and nine pence Three pounds per centum consolidated bank annuities arisi[ng]
    from Three thousand pounds Sterling lodged the Eleventh day [of]
    April one thousand eight hundred and thirty seven in the Bank of En[gland]
    at the price of Ninety and three fourths per cent and placed in [trust]
    the same day on account of Miss Susanna Churchill in the n[ames]
    of the said Colonel Cerjat and De Palezieux Falconnet my [agents]
    appointed.

  B Of the sum of Five hundred pounds Sterling which I the
    Viscount Melbourne shall place at the disposal of Miss Susan[na]
    Churchill towards her personal expences on the occasion of [the]
    Marriage as also towards the expences of their house[hold]
    Establishment.

Third That the clauses and conditions stipulated in the Trust of
  Churchill's Fortune (which is stated in A above) are established to [produce]
  their effect when it may be necessary.

Fourth That unforeseen and unprovided for circumstances affect[ing the]
  interests of the said intended husband and wife shall be governed by the
  code of the Canton of Vaud under which the Marriage Contract [will]
  be framed.

Fifth – Finally the office which I confer upon my said Attornies [has]
  also for its object that they may see that the provision made for [...]

Aimé Cuénod the Husband by the Reverend Mr Jean Samuel Cue his Father may be secured by the Marriage Contract conformably his Power of Attorney delivered twenty seventh February one thous eight hundred and thirty seven.

By means of which will be accomplished the object of the pres Power of Attorney taking to myself the whole charge and responsibi which may result from it, promising to agree to all which the said Messi Colonel Corjat and Aimé de Palezieux, shall do in my name, to who I give full power to act and to represent me — Also in case of n I consent that my said Attornies may substitute any other pers whom they shall think proper to act in their name and more for fulfilment of these Presents on the aforesaid terms and conditions.

Thus signed sealed and delivered at London in the form English law so that these Presents may be authentic the four day of April one thousand eight hundred and thirty seven.

Signed sealed and delivered
the said William Lord
count Melbourne in the
ence of   Melbourne

M: Coverdale

Solicitor, Grays Inn
London.

Lord Melbourne's power of attorney to Susan's two Swiss trustees on her marriage is shown here and on the previous page 'Signed sealed and delivered by the said William Lord Viscount Melbourne . . .' at Gray's Inn (Archives cantonales vaudoises).

100

Susan Churchill could have learnt her true parentage only from Lord Melbourne, and perhaps also from Lord Bessborough. They, in 1836 and 1837, were the only people left who were involved in the events surrounding Susan's birth in March 1818. Lady Bessborough and Lady Caroline Lamb, who would have known where — and whether — she had been baptised, were dead; her own mother Harriet von Westerholt must be presumed so by 1836; her grandfather William Spencer had died in 1834; her grandmother Mrs Spencer was living in Germany and was in poor health; and her Churchill grandparents had never played any (traceable) part in her life. What, then, was Susan told? A long time later, in 1848, a few months before the death of Lord Melbourne, she wrote a memorandum at the end of the book containing her journal. She wrote it for her children, not, she said, because the sad story could be of any use or advantage to them, but simply because they would doubtless one day be interested in their mother's history. It is a dignified and touching document. Written in French, because by the date of the memorandum, 11 March 1848, she had wholly adopted her husband's language, she says [in translation]:

. . . My mother was the daughter of The Hon. William Spenser [sic] son of Lord Charles Spenser, the youngest son of the deceased Duke of Marlborough, or Malbrouke as the French call him [this of course is a reference to the French folksong 'Malbrouke s'en va-t-en guerre'.] and of Mrs. Spenser . . . My father is the Duke of Marlborough.

She records her mother's subsequent married name, and says that she herself was born in London in March 1818. By 1848, when she wrote that information for her children, together with a record of the actions of Lady Bessborough and the Lambs, Lord Blandford had become the sixth Duke of Marlborough. She could hardly have been given this information about her parents if, for example, her father had been Henry de Ros, as Mrs Arbuthnot had alleged, or her mother had been the Miss Susanna Adelaide Law of the baptism certificate.*

Susanna Adelaide Law, mother of the child Susanna Churchill of the St Marylebone baptism entry which was copied for Lord Melbourne, was therefore not Susan's mother. If, however,

---

*See the Appendix for a more detailed discussion of the relationship of Harriet Spencer and her daughter to both the fifth and the sixth Dukes of Marlborough.

Melbourne used that certificate as one of the documents needed for the marriage settlement (and Susan's marriage papers all carry the name of Susanna Churchill, not of Susan Harriett Elizabeth Churchill), he should not necessarily be accused of dishonesty. In 1836, 1837 and 1838 — though, for reasons to be explained, not later — he may really have believed that the entry referred to his ward. It was certainly not unknown, in cases where it was desired to conceal a child's true identity, for another woman to take the place of the mother in the baptismal record, or even for the entry in the register to omit one or both parents' names altogether. This happened in the case of Horatia Nelson, the daughter of Nelson and Lady Hamilton. She was baptised in that same church, St Marylebone, in 1803 when she was over two years old, and her name (recorded as Horatia Nelson Thompson — the last being a fictitious name invented by her parents) was entered with those of seven infants christened at the same time. Only Horatia's entry, however, appeared without any names of parents. Lady Hamilton had arranged that the officiating clergyman and the parish clerk should be paid double fees for this service.[7]

Further doubts concerning the St Marylebone entry of 1818 as identifying Harriet Spencer's daughter arise when the facts of the Blandford-Law affair are known, as in their general outline they are, and when they are seen in the context of the complex pattern of events and family relationships in 1817 and 1818.

*   *   *   *   *

THE AFFAIR ONLY became known to the general public in 1838, because of a libel action brought by Lord Blandford's family against a weekly paper called *The Satirist or the Censor of the Times*.[8]

The case contained subtle political undertones which reflected unhappy family relationships and rivalries among the Spencer-Churchills. It also had obvious moral overtones; and it had important implications for the Marlborough succession.

The political undertones of the suit were the result of a recent squabble in the Marlborough family over the local elections at Woodstock, Lord Blandford's constituency in which Blenheim Palace is situated. *The Age*, like *The Satirist* a widely read and violently scurrilous weekly, for political reasons supported the Tory Marquis of Blandford and, in issue after issue, could hardly find words strong enough to vilify his brother, Lord John Churchill, whom it called Black Parrot Jack, a reference to his naval career, and their father, the fifth Duke of Marlborough.

This was the Duke, father of the Marquis of Blandford and of Lord John and Lord Charles Churchill, who was known to be a political turncoat. He had, before entering the House of Lords, stood as a Whig for one constituency, and later as a Tory for another. Harriet Spencer's brother George, who had no reason to love his Churchill cousins, called the Duke his 'precious Cousin' when writing about these varying political allegiances; and he went so far as to add in confidence to his brother-in-law John Hobhouse, 'Between ourselves 'tis a poor beast, a very shambling animal'.[9] He had succeeded to the dukedom in 1817 and had obtained a royal licence to add the name of Churchill to that of Spencer, though when Mrs Arbuthnot, as usual accompanying the Duke of Wellington, visited him at Blenheim some years later and found him living like a recluse in a corner of the great house, she felt that he had brought only disgrace on the illustrious name of his ancestor the first Duke of Marlborough. (The name of Churchill had, for some generations, disappeared from the descendants of John Churchill, Queen Anne's great general, as the succession had gone to his daughter and hence collaterally to the Spencers.)

The attractive side of the fifth Duke's character was his passion for flower gardens — 'gardening mad', Mrs Arbuthnot called him — and for books and rare editions. Enormous debts drove him to sell his famous library, and he was involved in litigation when he was prevented from cutting down the trees of Blenheim which he wanted to sell for timber. His Will, and that of his wife (another Susan), were conspicuous in leaving nothing to their son George Spencer-Churchill, Marquis of Blandford, except a few pictures and a writing-table. Blenheim itself was of course entailed. All this is some measure of the unhappy relationships in the family of Susan's putative father.

The moral overtones of the libel action of 1838 appeared in the Judge's ruling at the end of the hearing. They are interesting, as showing something of the character and especially of the reputation of Lord Blandford. On the opposite side from *The Age, The Satirist* had attacked Lord Blandford with a wealth of invective which *Private Eye* might well envy today. *The Age*, from its political standpoint inadvertently, sparked off the case, because *The Satarist* picked up the story at which its rival had only hinted, and published it.

The Marlborough succession was involved because, by an Act of Queen Anne, the dukedom passes through the female line failing male issue, and this of course was the most serious aspect of the case, which was based on an allegation that Lord Blandford had committed bigamy and that consequently his heir, Lord Sunderland, and his other children were illegitimate; and further, that the daughter said to have been born to him and to Miss Susanna Adelaide Law in 1818 was the true heir.

Officially, the libel action was brought by Lord Blandford's son, the Earl of Sunderland. The story published by *The Satirist* was that in 1817 the Marquis had been living with a Miss Susanna Adelaide Law, daughter of a respectable merchant. The Marquis was alleged to have gone through a mock ceremony of marriage with her. The cruel deception which he practised on her in 1817 was admitted by him in the libel case of 1838. He promised to marry her, the story went, but explained to her that, 'for family reasons', the marriage must be kept secret. He would bring a clergyman to the house of her parents and there they would be married. Accordingly, on 16 March 1817, a marriage service was performed by a seemingly official clergyman, whom Lord Blandford introduced as his brother. This was indeed his brother, Lord Charles Churchill, but he was no clergyman. Miss Law later discovered that Lord Charles was an Army officer, and that she had been the victim of a trick marriage. There appeared to be no doubt at the trial in 1838 that she had at first believed that she was being properly married, though prosecuting counsel questioned whether her parents were equally taken in.

They then lived together in London, in various apartments near Baker Street, in the St Marylebone neighbourhood, and, somewhere around March 1818, a daughter was born. Miss Law, who had by then discovered that her 'marriage' was invalid, kept urging Lord Blandford to make her his lawful wife. He then arranged that they should spend the summer of 1818 in Scotland, where he would go for the grouse shooting in August, and she would take their infant, 'aged about four months', as the report of the trial noted. He was alleged to have promised that they would be married by public recognition according to Scottish law.

The whole case turned on whether they had in fact been publicly recognised in Scotland as man and wife. If they had, then

Lord Blandford's present marriage would have been invalid, his children illegitimate, and the daughter said to have been born in 1818 would be heir to the dukedom.

That this was no hole-in-corner affair but that they were known by Lord Blandford's friends to be living together in London is evidenced by the party which joined them on their journey to Scotland. They travelled separately until they reached the North. For a good part of the way, Miss Law was escorted by one of Lord Blandford's uncles, Colonel James Stewart, and by his cousin, who was later also to become his brother-in-law, Lord Garlies. In Edinburgh, they lived as Captain and Mrs Lawson, as they had in London; and during that summer Miss Law met others of Blandford's friends, notably Sir William Elliott and Lord Glenorchy. These were to be Blandford's two main witnesses in the libel action of 1838; they both swore that Miss Law had never been introduced to them in Scotland as Lord Blandford's wife, and Sir William Elliott claimed that he had booked lodgings in Edinburgh for Miss Law alone, not for 'Captain and Mrs Lawson', as the defendants alleged.

The prosecution also stated that Miss Law had eventually married, which she consistently denied: indeed it is difficult to see how she hoped to pin a charge of bigamy on Blandford if she had subsequently married in spite of believing herself to be his lawful wife. Lord Blandford had, during their association, been paying Miss Law a yearly allowance of £400. A point which no one disputed was that, up to about 1827, the Duchess of Marlborough, Lord Blandford's mother, had continued to pay this sum, through Coutts' Bank. At some stage, the allowance had been reduced to £200, when Miss Law had been compelled to surrender a number of letters which she held, some of them said to have been signed by Blandford as her 'husband'.

The case, which was tried in the Court of Queen's Bench, was known as Regina v. Gregory. Barnard Gregory was the publisher of *The Satirist*. The two counsel had been protagonists in the Norton-Melbourne divorce suit two years earlier: Sir William Follett, for Mr George Norton, now prosecuted Gregory; and Sir John Campbell, at this time Attorney-General, who had appeared for Melbourne, now defended Gregory and consequently Miss Law.

The most interesting of the three eminent lawyers was Lord Denman, then Lord Chief Justice. He was the principal Judge in the trial. Thomas Denman was a most sociable man, known to and greatly liked by a large circle of his contemporary Whigs, some of whom however thought more of him as an entertaining companion than as a great lawyer, in spite of his fame and popularity as the defender, with Lord Brougham, of Queen Caroline at her trial. Even his wit did not please everyone: Creevey found him no more than 'a feeble punster' at dinner, and criticised him for making inappropriate jokes in his Parliamentary speeches. Whatever may have been said about Lord Denman in the conversational ephemera of his day, his abiding memorial is his reforming work, in law reform and especially in his self-sacrificing labours for the abolition of slavery.

At the end of *The Satirist* trial, Lord Denman consulted with his fellow-judges on the bench, and then delivered a most remarkable ruling. It is difficult to know what to make of his speech. *The Satirist* lost the case: so much is clear. But when a judge, while not perfectly convinced, as he admitted, that one of the main defendants — Miss Law — had perjured herself, yet makes his decision mainly on grounds of compassion for the wife and children of the plaintiff, one can only wonder whether he was in advance of his time and was applying what would today be termed situational ethics rather than abstract justice, or whether Greville's stricture on his conduct of the Queen's Bench was true when he said that 'Denman has just law enough to lead him almost always wrong'.[10] Of Lord Blandford, Lord Denman said:

This is an application of a serious and interesting nature, both as regards the parties affected by it and as it relates to the principles on which we ought to administer justice with respect to criminal informations. I have not the least difficulty in saying, that if Lord Blandford alone had applied for this rule, I would never, for one, have consented to make it absolute; for, upon his own statement, a strong imputation is conveyed on his own conduct towards a respectable young lady. Her statements are certainly of a nature to create suspicion; but that some contrivances were resorted to, I have no doubt whatever, and I do not think that we would be justified in pronouncing them to be perjured. But Lord Blandford is not the only person to be considered: his wife and family complain of a libel which attacks them in their dearest interests and most tender feelings, and distinctly put[s] forward a series of imputations, with respect to which, I agree with the learned counsel who have supported the rule, that there is nothing in the affidavits on either side to show that such imputations are well founded. The Marquis of Blandford himself swears, that there was no marriage either in England or Scotland; and I do not find anything which, in fact, impeaches that statement.

Having said what he had about Miss Law's possible truthfulness, and balanced that by adding that he found nothing in Blandford's affidavit to impeach the Marquis' general statement, he concluded:

Considering, therefore, the interests of the individuals I have mentioned, and the importance of warning those who are disposed to traffic with character in this way that they cannot be allowed to do so with impunity, I think we are justified in saying, notwithstanding the misconduct of Lord Blandford, that Lady Blandford, the Earl of Sunderland, and the rest of the issue of this marriage, are entitled to have this rule made absolute.

There is nothing to lead one to suppose that, when Blandford proposed the Scottish marriage, Susanna Adelaide Law did not undertake that journey in good faith. All the facts which emerge from the Regina v. Gregory case in 1838 suggest that Blandford and she did live together in 1817 and 1818 — indeed neither this nor the mock marriage were ever denied — and that before the journey to Scotland they were thought by many people to be man and wife.

Although Miss Law herself is an unknown quantity, she yet gives the impression of having been a fairly simple, credulous girl, inexperienced enough in the ways of Lord Blandford's world to have put her faith in him and perhaps to have really loved him. The Judge's inclination not wholly to disbelieve her evidence is proof that, at the trial, she did not appear to the court to be a mercenary liar. Miss Law's father was a well-to-do provision merchant, originally from Dublin, who in 1817 was living in London, near Bryanston Square. Lord Blandford visited her there and gained her affection. When the proposed marriage was arranged, her family agreed to his condition of secrecy, and in 1817 the 'marriage' took place in a room in her father's house, with her parents and her sister (whose married name was given at the 1838 action) as witnesses. She was not yet seventeen. The only registration of the marriage was a note which her mother made on the fly-leaf of a prayer-book.

That was the gist of her affidavit. The name of her daughter — who was about four months old in August 1818, which would correspond with the baptism record of Susanna Churchill in St Marylebone church — is not mentioned in any of the trial reports of 1838. By that date, the daughter is said to be married to 'a gentleman of fortune', whose name is not revealed either. Yet this is the young woman for whom *The Satirist* and Miss Law were attempting to establish a claim to be in direct line of succession to the Marlborough dukedom.

When taxed with receiving the annual allowance paid to her by the Duchess of Marlborough, Miss Law said that she had looked upon it as a marriage allowance. She held to this claim although her association with Blandford ended after the episode in Scotland. He had insisted that it should cease, she said, because by the autumn of 1818 he was about to marry. Miss Law was seriously ill for some weeks as a result.

Five years after the break-up of their relationship, they met again. By then he had been married for four years. This is *The Satirist's* report of Miss Law's affidavit: '[After five years] he called on her in Fludyer Street, Westminster, and on his knees implored her to forgive his past conduct and admitted his baseness. She then declared he was her husband, that although he had married another, she had not. That [he] admitted the fact, and that she . . . was his lawful wife, and urged in the most strenuous terms her return to him, which she refused, but, at his urgent request, agreed to meet him the following day at the house of his mother the Duchess of Marlborough. That [she] did not meet him, but wrote him a note declining the interview, to which note an answer in the following words was received . . . and is now in the possession of [her] solicitor:-'

October 29 (post mark 1823)

Reflection, reason, and a sincere regard for your welfare *now* and hereafter, these all conspire to convince me, dearest Susan, that I should not be justified in pressing your acquiescence to the step I meditated.
　　Therefore, dearest, consent to Charles's [Lord Charles, the 'clergyman' brother, doubtless] invitation: go there, and let us abandon all thoughts of the other plan. Take the little one to introduce her to her papa. I shall dine with Charles, and shall hope to meet you.[11]

This letter was read in court. Miss Law's affidavit ended with the assertion that she had not caused any statement to be inserted in *The Satirist*, and that during the last twelve months (i.e. between November 1837 and the date of the lawsuit, November 1838) she had been approached by a near relation of the Marquis of Blandford who had suggested that it would be to her advantage to seek an interview with the Duke of Marlborough's solicitor. Miss

Law had not done so. *The Satirist* was obliged to report that the 'near relation' was thought to be Blandford's brother, Lord John Churchill. *The Age* had already prepared the way for litigation by asserting, in June 1838, that it was in fact Lord John.

*   *   *   *   *

BEFORE ATTEMPTING TO answer the questions that spring to mind about events in 1817 and 1818 and about the motives for the libel action by Lord Blandford's family against *The Satirist* in 1838, it is useful to look at the sequence of dates and to consider what might precisely have caused the more scurrilous press to publish a series of statements in 1838 about a twenty-year-old scandal:

MARCH/APRIL 1836

Lord Melbourne has a search made for his ward's baptismal record. He receives the baptismal certificate (a copy of the entry in the register) for one Susanna Churchill, daughter of Miss Law and Lord Blandford. He consents to Susan's marriage.

SEPTEMBER 1836

The Swiss documents are ready for Susan's marriage.

APRIL 1837

Lord Melbourne gives his second consent. Susan Churchill's marriage settlement is drawn up, and trustees appointed.

JUNE 1837

Susan's marriage contract is signed.

AUGUST 1837

Susan marries in Switzerland.

JUNE 1838

The Age publishes a paragraph accusing Lord John Spencer-Churchill of approaching 'an individual who formerly lived with his brother . . .'

JULY 1838

The Satirist publishes three paragraphs on 'A Question of

Legitimacy' which implied a threat to the Marlborough succession: the libel.

The Duke of Marlborough, Lord Blandford's father, visits Lord Melbourne in Downing Street. This may be fortuitous or his visit may be connected with the libel and with the — to the outside world — now forgotten story of Harriet Spencer.

Lord Blandford, in the name of his heir Lord Sunderland, sues *The Satirist* for libel.

It is not unreasonable to suppose, when events are seen in that sequence, that certain journalists, always on the look-out for scandal, the daily bread of papers like *The Satirist* and *The Age*, got wind of Lord Melbourne's search in the parish registers, and found the St Marylebone entry. From there it would not have been difficult to work back twenty years to the liaison between Lord Blandford and Miss Law, but it could easily have taken a year to do it. *The Satirist* repeatedly said, before the case was heard, that the facts were known to few besides themselves, thus implying that they had unearthed an old scandal.

The press need have known nothing about Lord Melbourne's ward, Susan Churchill, in Switzerland, and this would be confirmed by the fact that there never was the remotest suggestion that Susan was a claimant to the Marlborough succession. But equally the action of the press in unearthing the Law scandal would answer the, at first sight, puzzling question why Miss Law waited twenty years before asserting herself to be Blandford's lawful wife. During those twenty years, the evidence suggested, even though she had not married, she had borne a number of children. For ten of those years, she had been deprived of at least half if not all of her allowance from the Duchess of Marlborough, and no doubt those who approached her in 1838 — whether it was the gutter press or Lord John Spencer-Churchill — were able to tempt her with promises of financial gain. All through the story, from her first meeting with Blandford when she was a girl of sixteen, Miss Law seems to have been used and manipulated quite unscrupulously.

Then there is the question of Lord Blandford's motives in

bringing the action. Could all the publicity, the broadcasting of his unsavoury past, the pain inflicted on his wife and children, have made it worth while for him to sue *The Satirist?* He might have been expected to ignore such a paper and to treat its reports with contempt. But in fact his past had, by 1838, caught up with him. By his mock marriage to Miss Law, probably by the long-term result of his seduction of Harriet Spencer (a daughter, now grown up and married in Switzerland, who might also come forward and claim that she was his child), and by his generally profligate conduct, he had made it virtually certain that at some point the validity of the Marlborough succession would be questioned. It had therefore become essential in 1838 to establish openly and at whatever cost the legitimacy of his heir.

Secondly, it was common knowledge that great bitterness existed between various members of the Churchill family, and if, as was alleged by the defendants in the case, Lord John had approached Miss Law and urged her to assert her claim to be the true Lady Blandford, it became all the more urgent and necessary to quash the rumours.

And last there was the press. People were terrified of the scandal-mongering papers, whose probing into privacy and publishing of defamatory stories had been increasing in recent years. The only way to disprove their reports and to clear one's character was to bring a libel action and hope to win it. A year or two before the Blandford-Law action, Henry de Ros, who had been accused of cheating at cards, not only sued his accuser but was said to be contemplating a libel action against *The Satirist*.[12] And a decade earlier, the Duke of Devonshire had complained, in connection with Harriette Wilson's *Memoirs* which had just appeared, of 'the licentious personalities of the newspapers'; and he added in brackets '(foolish to mind)'.[13] He, being on the whole an admirable young man, and unmarried, had little reason to mind; but for Lord Blandford's family any questioning of their legitimacy could have been a disaster and was bound to rake over old scandals.

The crucial question raised by the St Marylebone baptism of Susanna Churchill in 1818 has to be looked at on the basis, first, of such facts as can be gathered; and secondly of the social and moral aspects of Lord Blandford and his circle in 1817 and 1818.

Put simply, the question is this: are there in reality two children, with the same Christian name, fathered by the same man, both born in the same month of the same year?

If there was only one, then she was Susan Harriett Elizabeth Churchill, Lord Melbourne's ward, for she is known to have existed and her childhood, youth and later life are sufficiently documented. But any record of her baptism, which might have been expected to show the names of her parents, is missing. If, as seems likely, she was baptised, the fact would have been known only to Lady Bessborough and to her daughter Caroline Lamb. This in turn raises the much more questionable notion of whether the St Marylebone baptism was indeed hers, with Miss Law's name substituted for that of Miss Harriet Spencer, and her full Christian names unrecorded in this surreptitious ceremony. That Lord Melbourne, in 1836, obtained a copy of the baptism entry is a fact; that he used it as one of Susan's marriage documents is a surmise, based on the change from Susan to Susanna, and on the date of its being copied coinciding with the preliminaries to her marriage.

On balance, however, the available evidence in this mysterious affair suggests that there were two children. The weaker side of this argument is that Miss Law and her daughter let twenty years go by without claiming any recognition; and, more important, that at the court hearing in 1838 the daughter is a very shadowy figure indeed in the background of Miss Law's affidavit. She does not appear in person, her name is not given, and the 'gentleman of fortune', her husband, is mentioned almost casually as bringing forward her claim to the Marlborough succession. The stronger evidence for the existence of Susanna Churchill is, first, that Lord Blandford in 1823 wrote to Miss Law asking her to take 'the little one' to a rendez-vous at Lord Charles Churchill's house and that by then Susan is known to have been with the Lambs; and secondly that at the court hearing Lord Blandford admitted to living with Miss Law and did not deny that there had been a child who was about four months old when they all travelled to Scotland in August 1818.

The similarity in the names of the two children presents no problem: Miss Law's first name was Susanna, and the Christian name of both Susan's grandmothers was also Susan. If there were two children, then, on the present assumption, each is named after a parent or grandparent.

There one must leave such factual parts of the story as can be known. As to the social and psychological aspects of the connection between George Spencer-Churchill and his cousin

Harriet Spencer, in 1817, it is only by trying to penetrate the relationships of the families concerned, all the complexity of individual lives, the interweaving of social, economic, and political factors, and the contemporary influences which bore on them, that something of the essential truth underlying the puzzle may be surmised.

In the search for truth, the explanation given to Susan herself and repeated by her in her 1848 note to her children must be considered from two aspects. Having identified her parents as Harriet Spencer and 'the Duke of Marlborough', she explains that 'while still very young, my poor mother became pregnant without being married.' As she and 'the Duke' were of the same social standing (she uses the French word 'rank' which has a slightly different connotation in English), 'he should have married her, but the Lord did not allow that marriage to take place'.

All this tallies with the assumption that Blandford was her father, as he was certainly still single in 1817, though a number of people thought that his marriage to Miss Law in that year was valid. That may indeed be one of the reasons why it was thought best that Harriet and he should not marry. But it is the rest of the story which seems improbable, though clearly Susan herself always believed it to be true. Susan, so she records in her memorandum, was told that her father had fought a duel, and that her mother's parents had forbidden their daughter Harriet Spencer to marry him, fearing lest she should be unhappy, married to a duellist. This must surely have been a tale concocted by Lord Melbourne, and perhaps by Lord Bessborough, to bolster her own self-respect. When and where was such a duel fought? There is so far no traceable record of it in any year of Lord Blandford's adult life. Did William Spencer fight his younger cousin to defend his daughter's honour? Spencer certainly was the only one of Thomas Moore's friends to own pistols when Moore borrowed them for his farcical duel with Francis Jeffrey of *The Edinburgh Review*. It was not unheard of for a girl's father to engage her lover in a duel. Readers of Jane Austen's *Pride and Prejudice* — in which the social mores are contemporary with those of Susan's parents — will remember that Mrs Bennet feared that her husband would feel obliged to challenge Wickham who had eloped with Lydia Bennet; Lydia had no brothers to 'step forward' in circumstances where 'loss of virtue in a female is irretrievable . . . one false step involves her in endless ruin'. Such dramatic action as a challenge hardly sounds like William Spencer. Nor unfortunately does the explanation of the girl's parents preventing the marriage so as to safeguard her future happiness tally with what is known of Mrs Spencer. It is true that she suffered greatly when the disaster of Harriet's pregnancy became a matter of public knowledge; but that kind of pain apart, she might in other circumstances well have been capable of cherishing ambitions to make her daughter Harriet the future Duchess of Marlborough.

Lord Blandford himself, who, according to the line of argument which must credit him with two illegitimate daughters, plays such an important but remote role in the events which ultimately led to Lord Melbourne's having the responsibility for the welfare and happiness of Susan Churchill, is a difficult person to delineate with any sureness. For a man whom *The Satirist* could pillory week after week for the lowest kind of debauchery, the life of George Spencer-Churchill seems to have gone largely unrecorded, except on two points — his looks, and one glorious political moment in the House of Commons.

He possessed great physical beauty. This was attested to by one of his Eton school-fellows, who also said that he had been a ringleader of what became known as the Keate riots at Eton. The first of these riots occurred in 1810, when George Spencer, Lord Sunderland, as he was then, had been at Eton for five years. The cause of the riots was the flogging first of twenty boys who had disobeyed the orders of the headmaster, John Keate, to behave quietly in the antechapel, and then of sixty more boys who had thrown rotten eggs at Keate.

Throughout his political career Blandford, unlike his father, was a consistent Tory. He was returned as Member for Chippenham at the very height of the crisis in his personal affairs, on 4 August 1818 — a matter of days therefore before his grouse-shooting expedition to Scotland with Miss Law. Later, he was three times Member for Woodstock, and it was in the last of these elections, in 1838, that the personal and political feud with his brother reached its height. Lord John contested Woodstock as a Whig, against his brother Blandford. The attack on Blandford by the pro-Whig *Satirist* in that same year therefore has political significance, and any scandal, even a twenty-year-old one, that could be unearthed in order to blacken his character would have been a gift to that paper.

Lord Blandford's parliamentary activity comes as a slight

surprise in the light of his apparently shallow character and of his Toryism; and, during the years of debate which culminated in the Reform Bill of 1832, he proved something of an embarrassment both to his own side and to the traditional reformers. He had been roused to take up the cause of Reform by his hatred of the Catholic Emancipation legislation, which he felt had been carried against public opinion, by Members of Parliament who were unrepresentative of it — this unrepresentative nature of Parliament being of course the essence of the reformers' cause. ' . . . And from that moment', reported the *Annual Register*, 'he had become a fiery and reckless reformer, frequently forcing forward the question against the wishes and advice of its longer tried and more experienced patrons, and never distinguished by moderation in his schemes'. He spoke in the debate in 1829, when Wellington was Prime Minister, and got the support of some Whigs, including John Hobhouse who was teased by a 'waggish' Peel for his conversion to the other side of the House. Blandford's Bill for parliamentary Reform was a curious mixture advocating a return to what he conceived to be true democratic principles according to his reading of constitutional history, and some startling new ideas, for instance that Members should be paid an attendance allowance. This last drew some comments of amused contempt from his own Tory Home Secretary, Peel. Even the debate and the final voting was confused; the reformers, in Opposition, did not know how to deal with what the *Annual Register* reported as 'the Marquis' most crude and unintelligible proposal', and wanted to substitute for the Bill a generalised resolution on Reform. But according to Hobhouse, the Whig reformers 'by some unaccountable confusion . . . voted for Blandford's Bill . . . '[14], which however was lost.

An interesting aspect of Blandford's Bill was the whole-hearted support given to it by the Birmingham Political Union. This was a Radical body, which was able to organise massive demonstrations in favour of Reform; its leadership was intelligent and thoughtful, and had been particularly attracted by that part of Blandford's Bill which dealt with ancient constitutional rights of electors. At the time of the Regina *v.* Gregory case in 1838, *The Satirist*, if it can be believed, reported that Blandford had subsequently been 'kicked out of' the Birmingham Political Union.

The impression left by the few facts of Blandford's recorded life is of a man who acted on impulse, unrestrained alike in his selfishness and in his enthusiasms, and possibly not of any particular intelligence. When he died, as sixth Duke of Marlborough, in 1857, the serious newspapers could find — or perhaps wished to find — absolutely nothing to say about him in their obituaries, and contented themselves with tracing his genealogy back to his famous ancestor, John Churchill, first Duke of Marlborough. But Lord Denman's strictures leave little doubt as to his general reputation in his youth.

That youth, like that of the men glimpsed around Miss Law and around the Spencers in 1817, was spent during the Napoleonic wars. These men, two years after Waterloo, were mostly in their early twenties. The younger generation, of which Caroline Lamb was an older member, differed from the generation of Lady Bessborough and her sister Georgiana, not in being less moral in their sexual behaviour but in being less discreet about it. This was obviously true of Caroline Lamb in her affair with Byron, and it seems to have been sadly true of Harriet Spencer some years later.

Most of the young bachelors of the 1817 story were noted for their excesses and for their profligacy. A number of them had been contemporaries at Eton. Cruel practical jokes they thought amusing, and Lord Blandford's mock marriage to Miss Law was not the only farce that was played out, to the intense suffering of the victims. In society many of them were attractive because of their wit and ability to entertain and to gossip. A sharp difference between the love affairs of Devonshire House at the turn of the century, and those of Blandford and his contemporaries, was that now even unmarried girls were the subject of anecdotes linking their names with these young bachelors. Harriet Spencer's was linked with Henry de Ros and (probably George, not his younger brother) Wombwell, both contemporaries in age and at Eton with George Spencer-Churchill, an indication that he was one of their circle. But Harriet was not alone. Later, Caroline Lamb wrote to her husband, when clearly they had been discussing old rumours concerning Susan, who was then at Brocket, that she could not remember who had told her but that she had a clear recollection 'that Henry de Roos [sic] assisted by Ld Alvanley and others had seduced away a very handsome and innocent young girl whom L^y Salisbury was bringing up under her maid . . . '[15]

Miss Law, having been a respectable girl though not in the same social world as Harriet Spencer, had lost her respectability after her supposed marriage. Her escorts on her Scottish journey were friends and, apart from his uncle Colonel James Stewart, contemporaries of Blandford, and at that time all unmarried. It was due to the witness of two of them in 1838 that Blandford won his libel action; and although they swore that Miss Law had never been recognised as his wife in Scotland, nevertheless they were part of the group, like his brother Lord Charles who had performed the earlier 'marriage' ceremony, who aided and abetted Blandford in his affair.

That Harriet Spencer and Susanna Adelaide Law were apparently seduced by Blandford at the same time is a doubtless horrifying example of debauchery. An association with Harriet Spencer simultaneously with one with Miss Law would, had the former come out at the 1838 trial, have been seen to be so dishonourable as to have called for even severer condemnation by Lord Denman. But of course it was not known, and it must in fairness be said that we do not know the other side of the case nor the provocation that Harriet's behaviour may have presented. Their relationship could well have been not an association but a sudden seduction, as might happen for example at a ball. The intoxicating waltz was still in vogue then, less than a decade after Caroline Lamb had danced it with such joy until Byron's lameness stopped her; it was the first dance to bring the partners into close physical proximity, and was thought by many to inflame the passions; and it was consequently banned by some hostesses from their ballrooms. Harriet in turn may have been overcome by her cousin's great personal beauty. The waltz and a handsome man may be the simple explanation of Harriet's tragedy.

By the time that Harriet's pregnancy became so unusually widely known, Blandford was in a serious scrape. He was pretending to be married to Miss Law, living with her in London, and now was about to become the father of her child, and (judged by Susan's note on her parents), also of his cousin Harriet's. His family meanwhile were in increasing financial difficulties. His father, the fifth Duke, was preparing to sell the wonderful library which he had collected at his property of White Knights, near Reading; early in 1819 it was auctioned. A valuable edition of Boccaccio's *Decameron*, which he had bought for £2,260 in 1812, was sold for only £875 to Lady Bessborough's brother. And it was at that time that he tried to sell the trees at Blenheim. It was necessary therefore that the Marlborough heir should marry well. An alliance with the William Spencers was scarcely suitable in the circumstances — William himself penniless and having lost much of his former popularity, his wife discredited by her own behaviour and by her lack of care for her daughter, and Harriet now the subject of a public scandal. And if Blandford were to marry Harriet, and the child soon to be born were to be a girl, she would be the legitimate heir to the dukedom, at least until the birth of a son.

After his break with Miss Law, there was much speculation about Blandford's expected marriage. He was rumoured to be about to marry Lord Breadalbane's daughter, sister of one of his companions in the Scottish episode. Then, the matchmakers said, he was going to marry Lady Elizabeth Conyngham, whose mother was the powerful court favourite of George IV. In January 1819, he married Lady Jane Stewart. She too was a cousin, the daughter of the Earl of Galloway — doubtless a suitable marriage from his parents' point of view. Lady Jane was sister of yet another of the young men in that August of 1818 in Scotland.

While the Marlboroughs in 1818 were trying to marry Blandford, the Spencers were endeavouring to find a husband for Harriet, and her marriage to her German cousin Charles von Westerholt eventually took place. Lady Bessborough had taken Harriet's baby, Susan Churchill, to her Roehampton house, and she and William and Caroline Lamb doubtless made themselves permanently responsible for the child — in any event they fulfilled this responsibility throughout their lives.

Seen thus, it becomes clear that these events are not disconnected, and it is fair to surmise that the link is the family relationship between the Spencer-Churchills, the William Spencers, and Lady Bessborough who had been a Spencer. Various members of the family may have disliked and despised one another; their styles were different and there were political and personal feuds. But when it came to the sort of crisis affecting Blandford and Harriet Spencer, there can be no doubt that agreement was reached by this triangle of families to conceal as far as possible the existence of Harriet's daughter and to arrange the respective marriages of Blandford and of Harriet. The Duchess of Marlborough undertook to pay Miss Law an allowance. It is to the immense credit of Lady Bessborough and of William and Caroline Lamb that Susan was not, as she might have been — and as it is rumoured that Horatia Nelson's twin was (unknown to Nelson) — put in the Foundling Hospital; that they took upon themselves the responsibility that should have been the William Spencers'; and that not one of them ever abandoned that trust.

*   *   *   *   *

THE THREAD WHICH ties these events together must also in some way be linked with the establishment of Susan's dowry at the time of her marriage in 1837. The question is who in fact provided the money for her settlement. Whether it was her father's or her mother's family is not known. The source of marriage dowries — much larger than Susan's — was often the cause of public curiosity. A young woman commonly thought to be the daughter of George IV was said to have had a settlement of £30,000 or £40,000: Lady Cowper was greatly exercised at being unable to make out where the money came from. The recent loss of the correspondence about Susan's marriage trusteeship has been mentioned (see the Preface); but it is possible that other family papers relating to Harriet and her daughter Susan were destroyed by the Spencers themselves. When Caroline Lamb died, Harriet's brother George Trevor Spencer was concerned about Caroline's papers and made enquiries about them. Of course at that time most enquirers wanted to know how far any of Caroline's letters might embarrass those nearest to Byron; but George Spencer was much more likely to have been worried about any documents concerning his sister's history and that of her child. All Lord Blandford's personal papers were destroyed at his death, on his own instructions given when he was sixth Duke of Marlborough.

One certainty there is, however: Lord Melbourne, who had inherited the fulfilment of the responsibility for the girl from his mother-in-law and his wife, years after their death, discharged his responsibility to his ward with whole-hearted generosity.

Between Melbourne's 1836 consent to the marriage and the second one of April 1837, Susan's marriage settlement was being worked out. It was complicated by the fact that her prospective family were in Switzerland, while her guardian and her blood relations — supposing they were involved — were in England. Lord Melbourne therefore gave his power of attorney to two men who, like so many Swiss before and since, travelled continually for business or diplomatic reasons between the two countries. One of them, Colonel Charles Sigismond Cerjat, belonged to an Anglo-

Swiss family and had served in the British Army. The other, Pierre de Palézieux Falconnet, had business interests in England. These two were empowered by Melbourne to act as Susan's trustees in Switzerland. The other trustees, in addition to Melbourne himself, were Lord Bessborough and his youngest son William Spencer Ponsonby, later Lord de Mauley, both of whom had so faithfully befriended Susan throughout her life. Melbourne attended to all this at one of the most momentous times in his life, during the last months of William IV; Queen Victoria came to the throne on 20 June 1837.

The sum put in trust was considerable for the dowry of an unknown girl at that time: over three thousand pounds in 3% Consols was placed in the Bank of England in a joint account opened in the names of Cerjat and de Palézieux.[16] Lord Melbourne added £500 of his own for Susan's personal expenses on her marriage and towards establishing her new home. This money was to be at her own disposal. There is something a little sad about the fact that it was her schoolmistress, Mademoiselle Mange, who helped her to buy her trousseau: it so poignantly highlights the girl's lack of family and close friends.

But never again was Susan to be lonely: in fact she may sometimes have wished for a little more solitude to share with her husband: after the cut pages in her journal, which create a gap of twenty months, her first entry was:

We were married at Prilly at 12 o'clock the 9th of August 1837. There was a breakfast at Epenex . . . we set off for Vevey at 7 in the evening my mother in law & sister [in-law] Louise accompanied us we arrived at Vevey at 11 only because the horses went so slowly.

NOTES

1. Panshanger MSS, Box 37, Mrs Caroline Norton to Lord Melbourne, April 1836.
2. A traditional saying handed down in the Cuénod family.
3. Archives cantonales vaudoises, Etat-Civil, Prilly, 1837, No. 23.
4. ibid., Dg 122/1.
5. Greater London Record Office, St Marylebone Parish Register of Baptisms, 1818.

6. Lamb Papers, Melbourne Hall, Derbyshire.

7. *Horatia Nelson*, Winifred Gérin.

8. For the accounts of the Regina *v.* Gregory libel action, and for references in this text see: *The Times; The Morning Post; The Satirist or the Censor of the Times; The Age; Annual Register* — all for 1838. *The Complete Peerage*. Vol. VIII. footnote under 6th Duke of Marlborough. *Law Reports: The Revised Reports*, 47, 1837-1839, *Reports of Cases Argued and Determined in the Court of Queen's Bench*, Adolphus and Ellis, Vol. VIII, 1838. See also *The Later Churchills*, by A. L. Rowse.

9. British Library Add. MSS., Broughton Papers, 36, 463, f. 387, the Rev. George Trevor Spencer to John Cam Hobhouse [1827].

10. *The Greville Diary*, edited by Philip Whitwell Wilson.

11. *The Satirist or the Censor of the Times*, 25 November 1838.

12. This is alleged by Sydney Smith in his *Letters*, but as their editor, Nowell C. Smith, says, it cannot be verified as there are no copies of *The Satirist* for 1836 in the British Library.

13. Devonshire MSS, Chatsworth, 6th Duke's Group, 767.449. 1825.

14. *Recollections of a Long Life*, Lord Broughton.

15. Panshanger MSS, Box 17, Caroline Lamb to William Lamb, 2 October 1827.

16. Bank of England, 3% Consols Stock Ledgers 14, 15 and 16.

EPILOGUE

. . . If you were to turn Tory why I should turn
also . . . but I see my political confessions are leading
me rather too far so adieu dear Lord Melbourne.

letter from Susan to Lord Melbourne, 1841[1]

SUSAN WAS DOING herself an injustice when she once
wrote to her guardian, 'You will say that I am never contented and
that when I have one thing I always want another'.[2] Hers was not a
discontented nature. She enjoyed life, and responded warmly to
the slightest offer of affection. Her married life was happy and
serene. She and Aimé Cuénod lived in Vevey, in a house in the
Grande Place, the large market square with a shore lapped by the
Lake of Geneva. They had ten children in seventeen years, two of
whom died in infancy. The two eldest surviving children were
called Caroline and William, the latter in its English version: and so
her gratitude to her guardians was recorded by their names. Susan
was often surprised at the ease with which she gave birth to her
children, being well and active up to the last hours of her
pregnancies. She worried about the suitability of local nurses, and
loved her children devotedly.

On at least one occasion, in 1844, she paid a visit to England. She
kept in touch with Melbourne. She hoped he would approve of her
having whipped Caroline for hurting a dog. She gave him news of
old friends, particularly of Lady Brandon who was still living in
Geneva, lonely since Lilly's marriage. And Lord Melbourne kept in
touch with her. In 1841, within weeks of the fall of his government,
when he knew that his Indian summer as Victoria's Prime Minister
was probably over for good, he told Susan to write to him
whenever she felt inclined. Sometimes her own friends like
Thomas Jeans came to Vevey to see her. But tranquil and happy

Aimé and Susan Cuénod's house at Vevey is seen on the right between the pillars.

Another view of Vevey. The Cuénods' house is hidden by the castle on the left which was replaced by the turreted building shown in the other picture.

though her life was, it was by no means dull and uninteresting. There was more occupy her than the social round of the small town, even with its many English visitors. Although Lausanne was the Swiss lake-side resort most visited by the English, Vevey had for many generations been another. There were a number of Continental towns to which English ladies had gone in the past when they wished to conceal themselves for a time from the eyes of English society; Georgiana Duchess of Devonshire had gone to Aix-en-Provence for the birth of Charles Grey's child. Lady Elizabeth Foster was once thought to be behaving imprudently in 'Vevai', and the Duchess of Devonshire's chiding reveals the attitude which her generation held in such matters and puts one in mind of Harriet Spencer many years later, and even of Susan later still with Lady Brandon in Geneva.

. . . you had consented to go for one day with Mr. G. to Vevai and you allowed him to drive you out. This in itself is nothing, but suppose you had . . . seen a beautiful young woman arrive, travelling by herself, who, tho' there was nothing against her, had had imprudences laid to her charge, and that you saw this young woman giving parties and living with [this expression meant simply living in the same accommodation] two men, both suppos'd to be in love with her — with all your candour you would think her imprudent. I declare . . . I do not fear the *essential* with you one moment . . . but the opinion of the world . . . [3]

Susan gave some attention to Swiss politics, though her political views were always naive and some of her attempts at discussing public affairs with Lord Melbourne are almost irritatingly childish and ill-informed. In Geneva she had given no sign of reading the papers. But because of the missing pages in her journal, we cannot know whether she was aware that in 1836 the Swiss press were forecasting the imminent resignation of the British Prime Minister because of the impending Norton-Melbourne case.

Before she got to know her new country, she had written, rather touchingly, to Melbourne:

I am sorry I have no more political news to tell you but the Swiss are such *bons enfants* that one day both in their political & private life hardly ever differs from another.[4]

She remained a monarchist:

Now although I know full well you will not answer me a single word [she wrote to Melbourne after she had been married for four years], I must ask you what you think of poor Switzerland dont you think its going to rack and ruin with all its little bickerings and quarelling . . . the only thing I fear is my husbands being called out to fight for else I should rather like Switzerland to fall into the power of some other state to be governed by a King for I dislike Republiks indeed this hatred, & love of a Monarchy is my only political opinion.[5]

In the last resort, her political allegiance was tied to her affection for Melbourne:

When I am asked what I am I say Whig and have often battled for them for most of the English who come here are Tories — if you were to turn Tory why I should turn also . . . but I see my political confessions are leading me rather too far so adieu dear Lord Melbourne.[6]

Far from being naive in money matters, she had a keen business sense. Her interest in politics had begun to grow, she said later, because of the question of income tax, 'the tax upon fortunes . . . opinions nowadays appear to me to be playing at Puss in the corner for I think this a most radical idea and yet it comes from a Tory . . . the very same thing was voted *here* last year . . . and has succeeded very well although its very disagreeable.'[7]

Her marriage settlement had been most carefully worded so that her interests were safeguarded; and although Aimé Cuénod had certain rights to the money, the trust was so contrived as to protect Susan. By 1842 the couple were anxious to realise some of the stock held in her name by the Bank of England and to transfer the money to Switzerland. Susan consulted the trustee most easily available, Colonel Cerjat. But Lord Melbourne did not consider that it would be wise to move her capital, and he was concerned about the clause in the marriage contract which required that Aimé Cuénod should secure any sale of capital by an equivalent value in Swiss property. Susan understood all this perfectly, and she engaged in a lively though always respectful correspondence with Lord Melbourne. He had urged her to '*think* well' before selling any of her stock, but, she writes:

thought has not changed our wishes because it would be very useful to have 20 or 25 pounds a year more particularly now that we have two children but however Mr. Cuénod does not intend to urge it any further if you do not like it, although it was promised if he could give landed property as a guarantee. If you will give it to us we shall be very happy if not we will try and do without it so theres an end of it.[8]

But that was not the end of it. Melbourne replied immediately, and Susan hastened to assure him that her husband had no intention of 'speculating' with the money, for he agreed entirely with Lord Melbourne that such a practice was not safe and could not be approved. Susan then explained with great clarity that Mr Cuénod wanted to pay off what he still owed on his vineyards, and to use the balance of the money 'to lend to landed proprietors who mortgage their lands this is the general way of placing money here'. The interest would be of the order of 4 or 5 per cent, and these 'lettres de rente', Susan wrote, were considered exceedingly safe investments, so much so that 'my husband who has something to do with the *chambre de tutelle* generally places the orphans money in this way'. Mortgaged property should be worth three times the value of the loan, and Aimé made a little joke, hoping that his wife could trust him even though the security he offered — his vineyards and his mortgage holdings — was not worth quite as much as three times the money which he was asking Lord Melbourne to release. Susan continued the discussion in ever firmer terms, reminding Melbourne that her settlement promised '*the entire sum*' as soon as the security was agreed; but she again stressed that neither she nor Aimé would pursue the matter without his full consent. And 'Heigho! what a law letter I hope after all my trouble you will be able to understand it'.[9]

In the end, the stock was not sold until 1846, and the last thousand pounds was realised only in 1849, just after Melbourne's death. At this period, Susan and Aimé became the joint founders of a bank in Vevey. This was an unusual position for a woman in the nineteenth century. The bank was called the Cuénod-Churchill Bank of Vevey, and it was probably so called as much because of Susan's share in it, as because of the Swiss custom of adding a wife's maiden name to that of her husband. Aimé took to signing himself by the hyphened name Cuénod-Churchill.

Their eldest son William took over as owner-manager after his father's death, in 1882. Susan survived her husband by five years; the name Churchill was then dropped and the bank became Cuénod & Co. Towards the end of William Cuénod's life, he and his sons merged the business into the new Union of Swiss Banks. So both Cuénod and Churchill disappeared from the banking world.

Meanwhile Susan had undergone an important psychological change. 'Conversion', like Susan's and her husband's, to a deeply religious way of life, with its evangelical, fundamentalist language, was common to a good many mid-nineteenth century people who had grown up in the years before Queen Victoria came to the throne. Partly it was a reaction to the laxity in sexual mores of the earlier age; and partly it arose from the Romantics' dislike of the cool reason of eighteenth century theology and practice. In the field of religiously inspired morality, swings between periods of licence and of strictness are a commonplace of history. The Victorian age expressed itself with an effervescence and ardour which ranged from catholic revival to a multiplicity of evangelical groups, more and more fragmented as each one tried to get nearer to its notion of primitive Christianity.

The various protestant sects imposed their strict code of moral behaviour on their adherents. The alternative was to turn, not to the personally interpreted imperatives of the Bible but to the security and authority of Rome. This Louisa Spencer, Susan's aunt, had done, at a time, before the full flood of the Tractarian Movement, when few Anglicans went over to Rome, as the saying went. Such conversions were unusual enough for pious French families, some of them linked by marriage with the English aristocracy, to note with satisfaction when a young English girl found happiness in the Roman faith. Louisa was exceedingly devout, but in the sometimes rigid, innocently arrogant way of the convert. She wished, for example, that her friend Caroline Chinnery on her deathbed, which Louisa had to admit was a saintly one, had been granted the graces of the true faith before death. Louisa's strong attachment to various convents in France and in England, and to their Mothers — perhaps as substitutes for Mrs William Spencer, her own mother, and for a secure family life? — remained with her all her life. She recorded in her notebooks a number of sermons preached by well known French priests, and even published *A Short Treatise on the Cross*. Of her two clergyman brothers, one, George Trevor Spencer, later Bishop of Madras, came to hold evangelical views and played a bitter part in one of the major controversies, in the middle of the century, on eucharistic doctrine in the Church of England.

It was however no more than an accident of geography which first caused Susan and Aimé to come under the influence of John

Nelson Darby, very soon after their marriage. When still quite a young barrister, Darby had become convinced that ecclesiastical forms and denominational expressions of religion were contrary to the Christian gospel. For a time he joined a group of like-minded Brethren, who had met originally in Plymouth: they became known as the Plymouth Brethren. Later, dissensions arose, and a group hived off, calling themselves Darbyists. Before that happened, Mr Darby had gone to Lausanne on behalf of the Brethren, and there he gave a series of lectures on prophecy, in 1840. His hearers were so impressed that a number of congregations of Brethren sprang up, in Geneva and in Bern, but especially in Vaud, where Darby lived for some time. The congregations in Vaud, French-speaking and always of an independent mind, were later subjected to a certain amount of persecution. Susan's own ardent and freedom-loving nature would have responded to this with an even greater devotion to the cause. She and Aimé entertained Mr Darby in their home in Vevey, and were in every sense true converts. 'Blessed be the name of the Lord' became a refrain in her journal; and at least half the letter which Aimé left to his heirs about the disposition of his property consists of his thoughts on salvation. It is a simple and genuine expression of faith and as such is very moving. Aimé was, after all, a minister's son; but Susan had come a long way since saying, 'I am to be baptised and confirmed. How disagreeable'. Lord Melbourne, known to have thought that things would come to a pretty pass if religion were to invade everyday life, would have had little sympathy with his ward in her new-found faith; but by then their lives were widely separated.

Susan was fortunate that the man she fell in love with at a masked ball gave her forty-five years of contented married life. When she was a child, she was given a handsomely bound edition of *A Selection from the Papers of Addison*.[10] It looks, from the careful calligraphy on the fly-leaf, as if it were a school prize. It may be coincidence, but the ribbon marker — the book has scarcely been handled — has been left in the chapter on 'Love and Marriage' where these words occur: 'There is nothing of so great importance to us, as the good qualities of one to whom we join ourselves for life; they do not only make our present state agreeable, but often determine our happiness to all eternity'. This Susan truly believed. Her later journal, which she kept up for thirteen years after her marriage, is a happy, quiet account of the birth of her children, the

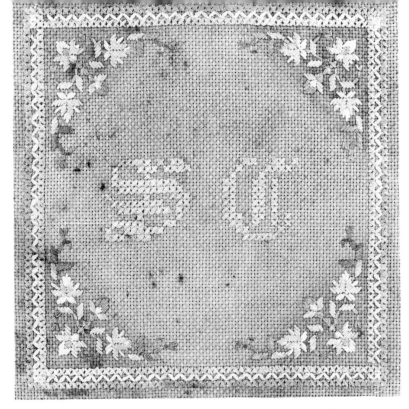

Embroidery done by Susan later in life and bearing her initials.

Susan Cuénod Churchill in the early 1880s, possibly the only photograph of her, and her husband Aimé Cuénod.

care which her 'dear Aimé' showed her, and her always-renewed gratitude to God for all the mercies which she felt had been showered upon her throughout her life.

She owed much in her life to her own strength and courage. Already as a child she had worked out a stoical attitude to sorrow, as she showed when those around her tried to warn her that the way would be hard after Lady Caroline's death, and later at her baptism in Lausanne. To cry was a most unusual thing with her, as she once recorded in her journal. Something of Lord Melbourne's own toughness may have permeated the atmosphere in which she spent her childhood at Brocket. He would not allow self-pity, least of all in himself; on being offered commiseration when his first government fell, he wrote that he had 'always thought complaints of ill-usage contemptible, whether from a seduced disappointed girl, or a turned out Prime Minister!'[11] That sentiment also shows something of the insensitivity that, for all his charm and honesty and, in the case of Susan, responsibility, still marks Melbourne's character.

But in the last resort, Susan owed everything to Lord Melbourne. Had he not kept faith with her, which really meant keeping faith with Caroline, completing what his wife had undertaken in rearing and educating Susan, and, by sending her to school in Geneva, giving her an educational opportunity well beyond the minimum required for girls, her story would at best have been that of a humble governess, utterly dependent on the goodwill of employers. Marriage would have been unlikely: respectable marriages without the backing of a family of substance rarely happened in the case of a 'child of the mist'. Georgiana Duchess of Devonshire, in her charity and kindness, hoped that her husband's daughter Charlotte Williams would marry a local squire, and Charlotte was considered fortunate when she married the nephew of the Devonshires' agent. True, there is no evidence of Melbourne's creating the possibility of a marriage for Susan; but she was not yet fifteen when she left England, and she was still a school girl when she met and married Aimé Cuénod. Caroline's Ponsonby family kept in touch with Susan, and in spite of Lady Brandon's remarks about them, their attitude suggests that, once Susan had finished school, they might well have given careful thought to her marriage opportunities.

And in the first instance, Susan owed everything to Lady Bessborough and to Caroline Lamb. Without them, her childhood would have been the usually miserable and always precarious existence of a girl orphan in the nineteenth century. From them she received that inestimable character-forming and happy gift: a secure early childhood. That gift enabled her to be the girl and woman she became — brave, facing life with humour and enjoying everything in it, even to the pleasure of 'speaking to the cows' on a country walk.

Lady Caroline brought her up as if she had been her own daughter, Susan was to write: and Lord Melbourne watched over her — even if distantly and unemotionally — till the end of his life. There is no doubt at all of their affection for one another: trusting and grateful on her side, faintly teasing and a little detached but none the less real on his.

William and Caroline Lamb's happiest times at Brocket were over before Susan went there. But she may have caught a whisper of those days, for she is best remembered as the girl with a great zest for life; and her own words still echo something of William and Caroline Lamb's younger and happier days: 'We had good fun and a bad dinner. We were very glorious'.

NOTES

1. Panshanger MSS, Box 17, Susan to Lord Melbourne, 26 August 1841.

2. ibid., August 1835.

3. *Georgiana. Extracts from the Correspondence of Georgiana, Duchess of Devonshire,* edited by the Earl of Bessborough.

4-9. Panshanger MSS, Box 17, Susan to Lord Melbourne, August 1835, 26 August 1841, 5 April 1842, 30 April 1842.

10. 1827 edition, in author's possession.

11. *Miss Eden's Letters,* edited by Violet Dickinson.

APPENDIX

'Who the devil knows who one's father is, anyway?'[1] Lord Melbourne thus sums up a whole aspect of Regency society with characteristic light-hearted cynicism. One cán make informed conjectures, based on available, but sometimes ambiguous, evidence and its interpretation, as this book has attempted to do for Harriet Spencer's child; equally, however, the numerous rumours running round Harriet in 1817 and 1818 must not be ignored. Mrs Arbuthnot stated categorically that Harriet's lover was Henry de Ros, and Maria Edgeworth on a later visit to London picked up some gossip about her having been seduced by 'a married man'.

A note made by Lord Ashley (who later became the seventh Earl of Shaftesbury of social legislation fame) in February 1828 in his *Journal* adds to the mystery while seeming to support Miss Edgeworth's statement. Writing from Woodstock, for which at that time he was Member of Parliament together with the Marquis of Blandford, he says:

Feb. 6th. — Woodstock. . . . Last night I dined with Duke of Marlborough. Never did I feel so touched as by the sight of his daughter, Susan — his natural daughter. She is Charlotte, our dear Charlotte, over again, in voice, in manner, in complexion, in feature, in countenance. I could hardly refrain from calling her *Sister*. O Great God, have compassion upon her forlorn state! What will become of this poor girl? What danger is she beset with? May *I* have the means of doing her some real lasting service? Father of mercies, grant Thy protection and keep her from the awful perils which are on every side.[2]

There are several reasons for giving careful consideration to Lord Ashley when he says that 'Susan' was the daughter, not of Blandford, but of his father the fifth Duke of Marlborough. Ashley was a member of the family: his mother was the Duke's sister, and one of his own sisters — older than himself — was called Charlotte. A family likeness between her and her cousin, an illegitimate daughter of the Duke, is perfectly natural. Two years later, in 1830, Lord Ashley was to marry Emily Cowper, Lord Melbourne's niece, so that he certainly became intimate with the family at Panshanger, neighbours and relations of the Lambs at Brocket. Other factors which might support the theory that the fifth Duke was Susan's father are the intense secrecy which surrounded her birth and childhood; the lack of any known explicit reference to Blandford in connection with Harriet; and Sir Harry Englefield's remark about Mrs Spencer's wishing to clear her daughter's character 'at least from the grosser & more distressing parts of the reports so prevalent against her . . . ' This last could be read to mean that her older, married cousin had been her lover — a 'gross' and shocking report.

It may seem surprising to find Susan at Blenheim Palace, and so it is, for never, in later reminiscences in her letters to Melbourne, does she mention any place but Brocket, and there is no suggestion in any of the documents, nor in her own note to her children, that she lived anywhere but there and, after Caroline's death, at school. But, since Ashley's testimony must be fairly looked at, there could be some significance in the date of his visit to Blenheim. Caroline had died on 26 January; and William Lamb could conceivably have sent Susan to the Spencer-Churchills, hoping that they would now assume responsibility for her. To find her there ten days after Caroline's death, however, seems improbable, though not impossible. Meanwhile, the Brocket household, through Mrs Peterson, was paying for Susan's 'mourning and board'.

Susan's memorandum to her children, detailing her parentage, may be ambiguous when read in the light of Ashley's comment; and yet she says, in 1848, 'my mother *was* . . . the daughter of William Spencer . . . etc.', and 'my father *is* the Duke of Marlborough'. She does however in a previous paragraph identify 'the deceased Duke' as the fourth (Blandford's grandfather) which could be taken to imply that she thought her father was the man who was the fifth Duke in 1818. But she goes on to say that her parents, both unmarried and of similar social background, should have married but were prevented from doing so because of the duel said to have been fought by her father, and she cannot be expected, in 1848 in Switzerland, to have known the precise chronological sequence of the Dukes of Marlborough. One cannot therefore with complete certainty distinguish, in what was told to her, between facts concerning the fifth and sixth Dukes of Marlborough, and what must surely, as in the story of the duel, be well-intentioned fiction.

And yet, having given due weight to Lord Ashley's statement, and looked at it in every possible light, there is something about the scene at Blenheim on that February evening of 1828 which does not ring true if it is really about Lord Melbourne's Susan.

At that date Susan would have been not quite ten years old. Lord Ashley's description of the girl at Blenheim is hardly that of a young child. 'Voice, manner, complexion, feature, countenance' were so like his own sister's, at that time already a married woman, that he wanted to call 'Susan' sister. An adult man does not normally think of an older sister as being in every way like a child of ten, but envisages her as she is in the present, not as he remembers her when he himself was even less than ten years old. And it is difficult somehow to imagine a little girl expressing a specific adult personality through her voice and manner.

Now the fifth Duke had an illegitimate daughter, Georgiana, who in 1828 would probably have been in her late twenties. She was the result of his affair at the turn of the century with Lady Mary Ann Sturt. There had been a *crim. con.* case about it in 1801. Again, no unwarranted assumptions must be made about the identity of the girl living or staying at Blenheim in 1828; but the 'forlorn state' and the 'awful perils' which aroused the interest of the man who became the archetype of a Victorian Evangelical are more likely to have applied to a grown young woman than to a little girl who would only have been glimpsed on a visit to Blenheim, notwithstanding Ashley's well-known interest in forlorn children.

The Duke had other natural children by various women. There was for instance the mysterious Miss Glover. In his Will, the Duke left all his goods and personal effects to 'Matilda Glover, now [1838] living in my family at Blenheim.'[3] She was the sole executrix and she inherited when the Will was proved in 1841. Earlier, she had lived, with other women, in one of the lodges of Blenheim Park. How long she had been there, and how many children she had, we do not know; but in his book *Oxford Common Room*, V.H.H. Green quotes a letter from a local inhabitant dated July, 1823. It gives a very garbled account of the comings and goings between Blenheim Palace and the lodge at all hours of the day and night, though it seems fairly clear that Miss Glover 'takes her eldest daughter' to the Palace every morning in the gig which the Duke had given her and fetches her back every night.

But the name Susan? Since it can be fairly well established that there was certainly more than one natural daughter, Lord Ashley could have made a genuine mistake, always supposing that this popular name had not also been given to one of these girls. When he visited his future family-in-law, the Cowpers, at Panshanger, he would doubtless have heard that at nearby Brocket the Lambs were bringing up an illegitimate Churchill child, Susan. Lady Cowper had herself recorded some years earlier that Susan had stayed in Brighton with William and Caroline Lamb. We know that Susan was not on close terms with the Cowpers, indeed may hardly have known them. Later, Lord Ashley may in all good faith have thought that the Duke's natural daughter whom he met at Blenheim was the Churchill girl of whom he had heard. And the fact that Susan's surname was Churchill and not some fictitious identity-concealing name is even more puzzling if she were the daughter of the fifth Duke, who in the circumstances would surely not wish her to be in any way identified as his child. His son however is more likely to have given the family surname to a daughter, as he certainly did in the case of Miss Law's child.

If Lord Ashley was so anxious to be 'of some real lasting service' to Susan, he might have been expected to have kept himself informed about her. Whenever Lord Bessborough and the William Ponsonbys went to Switzerland, they visited Susan. In 1833, Ashley with his wife and child, and his parents-in-law Lord and Lady Cowper, spent a week in Geneva. Susan was there at the time, but neither she nor they make any mention of having met.

Then there is the psychology of the thing. The Duke had had his share of notoriety in the general rakishness of his youth; but for this art-collector, garden-maker, turncoat politician, spendthrift and recluse, with a handy lodge in the Park, to have been the elderly lover of his cousin's young daughter, at a time when he was preparing to sell his precious collections, sounds a somewhat false note. It will be remembered that Harriet's brother George Trevor Spencer was married to a sister of John Cam Hobhouse, the Whig politician and friend of Byron. In 1825 Hobhouse received two delightful letters from the Duke of Marlborough, inviting him to Blenheim and wishing to discuss a letter from one of Hobhouse's sisters — almost certainly Mrs George Spencer, whose letters figure in the Hobhouse correspondence at this time.[4] It is unlikely that the Duke would have been on such terms with any relations of the William Spencers, in spite of George Spencer's political opinion of him as a 'poor beast', if he, as head of the family and a married man, were Harriet's seducer. The same goes for the Duchess, who in her Will left small gifts to two of William Spencer's daughters-in-law.[5] Harriet herself was involved with a group of young men who, according to Sir Harry Englefield, were besmirching her reputation and were themselves so much at fault that they should in honour not have mentioned her.

The strongest indications in favour of the reasoning detailed in these pages are Susan's own words, and the Blandford-Law baptism certificate. There is no doubt that Susan always believed what she had been told: that her parents were both single at the time of her conception, and that nothing, legally or socially, prevented their marrying. Her reference to 'the Duke' as her father, therefore, clearly means the man who became the sixth Duke in 1840, because that man — Lord Blandford — was single in 1817. The fifth Duke, his father, was married and the Duchess of Marlborough was still alive. But Susan had to be given some explanation as to why her parents had not married. If her father had been the fifth Duke, no explanation was necessary, because as a married man he could not have married Harriet Spencer.

Then there is the undeniable fact that Melbourne obtained the Blandford-Law baptism certificate and used it — at least to the extent of calling his ward Susanna, the child described as Blandford's daughter in the certificate, and not Susan Harriett Elizabeth, in her marriage documents. Melbourne, as Lady Bessborough's son-in-law and Caroline Lamb's husband, must have known the identity of the father of the child whom they — and he — cared for from her birth until they died.

Some of the mystery surrounding Susan still remains until further evidence turns up. When all has been said, does it matter? Very probably not, because the uncertainty does nothing to alter the point of the story and the reason for telling it: that the child, born amid grief, gossip and mystery, became a delightful person whose whole life is a tribute to the sense of responsibility and the affectionate care of Lady Caroline Lamb and of Lord Melbourne.

NOTES

1. Quoted in *The Later Churchills,* A. L. Rowse.
2. *The Life and Work of the Seventh Earl of Shaftesbury, K.G.,* Edwin Hodder
3. Public Record Office, Will of the 5th Duke of Marlborough, January 42 − 1841.
4. British Library Add. MSS, Broughton Papers, 36.461, ff. 247, 249, September 1825.
5. Public Record Office, Will of Susan, Duchess of Marlborough, May 353 − 1841.

BIBLIOGRAPHY AND SOURCES
OF REFERENCE

Airlie, Mabell, Countess of — *In Whig Society; Lady Palmerston and her Times.*

Arbuthnot, Mrs — *The Journal of Mrs Arbuthnot,* edited by Francis Bamford and the Duke of Wellington.

Bach, E., and Bridal, G. A. — *Lausanne. Promenades historiques et archéologiques.*

Baumgarten, Sandor — *Le Crépuscule néo-classique: Thomas Hope.*

Beauclerk, Lady Diana — *Letters from 1797 to 1807.* Privately printed in Heidelberg.

Bessborough, Earl of (editor) — *Lady Bessborough and her Family Circle; Georgiana. Extracts from the Correspondence of Georgiana, Duchess of Devonshire.*

Bickley, Francis (editor) — *The Diaries of Sylvester Douglas, Lord Glenbervie.*

Blandford, The Marquis of — Bill for Parliamentary Reform, as proposed by the Marquess of Blandford in the House of Commons, Feb. 18, 1830, with the Declaration of the Birmingham Political Council thereon. (British Library).

Boy Scouts Association, published by — *The Gilwell Book.*

Broughton, Lord (John Cam Hobhouse) — *Recollections of a Long Life.*

Bulwer, H. L. — *Private Memoir of the late Lord Melbourne.*

Cecil, Lord David — *The Young Melbourne; Lord M.*

Cerjat — *La Maison de Cerjat.* Privately printed in Switzerland.

Constant, Charles de — *Le Causeur, 1832.* (Archives de Genève). *Chronique sociale de Genève.* (ibid.)

Craven, Mrs Augustus — *Récit d'une Soeur.*

Creevey — *The Creevey Papers,* edited by John Gore.

Croft-Murray, Edward — *Decorative Painting in England. Vol. II.*

Cuénod, Alexandre — *Chronique de la Famille Cuénod.*

Eden, Emily — *Miss Eden's Letters,* edited by Violet Dickinson.

Edgeworth, Maria — *Letters from England 1813-1844,* edited by Christina Colville.

Gagnebin, Bernard (editor) — *Genève. Textes et Prétextes.*

Gérin, Winifred — *Horatia Nelson.*

Glenbervie, Lord — *Journals:* See Bickley, Francis and Sichel, Walter.

Greville, Charles — *The Greville Diary,* edited by Philip Whitwell Wilson. *The Greville Memoirs,* edited by Henry Reeve.

Gronow, Captain — *The Reminiscences and Recollections of Captain Gronow.*

Hawkins, Laetitia Matilda — *Memoirs, Anecdotes, Facts and Opinions.*

Haydon, Benjamin — *The Diary of Benjamin Robert Haydon.*

Hemlow, Joyce — *The History of Fanny Burney.*

Herold, J. Christopher — *Mistress to an Age: A Life of Madame de Staël.*

Hibbert, Christopher — *George IV, Prince of Wales, 1762-1811.*

Historical MSS Commission — 30 Fortesque X (W. R. Spencer to Thomas Grenville).

Hodder, Edwin — *The Life and Work of the Seventh Earl of Shaftesbury, K.G.*

Hoge, James and Olney, Clarke, (editors) — *The Letters of Caroline Norton to Lord Melbourne.*

Jenkins, Elizabeth — *Lady Caroline Lamb.*

Lamb, Charles — *The Works of Charles and Mary Lamb,* edited by E. V. Lucas. *Vol. VI, Letters, 1796-1820.*

Lambin, G. — 'Louis XVI angliciste': article in *Etudes anglaises,* April-June 1969.

Langley Moore, Doris — *The Late Lord Byron.*

Lascelles, E. C. P. — *The Life of Charles James Fox.*

Law Reports — The Revised Reports, 47, 1837-1839. Reports of Cases Argued and Determined in the Court of Queen's Bench. Adolphus & Ellis. Vol. VIII, 1838.

Lee, Robert — *Extracts from the Diary of the late Dr. Robert Lee, FRS. 1821-1822.*

Lever, Tresham — *The Letters of Lady Palmerston.*

Leveson Gower, Hon. F (editor) — *Letters of Harriet Countess Granville, 1810-1845.*

Leveson Gower, Sir G. (editor) — *Hary-o. The Letters of Lady Harriet Cavendish, 1796-1809.*

Leveson Gower, Lord Granville — *Private Correspondence 1781 to 1821,* edited by Castalia Countess Granville.

Lieven, Princess — *Correspondence of Princess Lieven and Earl Grey,* edited and translated by Guy Le Strange.
Letters of Dorothea, Princess Lieven, during her Residence in London, 1812-34, edited by Lionel G. Robinson.

Litchfield, Henrietta (editor) — *Emma Darwin: A Century of Family Letters.*

Lockhart, J. G. — *Life of Sir Walter Scott;*
Some Unpublished Letters: Notes & Queries, Vol. 187

Lyttelton, Lady Sarah — *The Correspondence of Sarah Spencer Lady Lyttelton,* edited by The Hon. Mrs Hugh Wyndham.

Marchand, Leslie A. — *Byron: A Biography.*

Marshall, William — *Extraordinary Trial! Norton v. Viscount Melbourne.*

Martin, William — *Histoire de la Suisse. Essai sur la Formation d'une Confédération d'Etats.*

Mitford, Mary Russell — *Recollections of a Literary Life.*

Monnier, Philippe — *La Genève de Töpfer.*

Moore, Thomas — *Memoirs, Journal and Correspondence.* edited by Lord John Russell.
The Poetical Works of Thomas Moore — Epistles, Odes and other Poems.

Morgan, Lady — *Lady Morgan's Memoirs: Autobiography, Diaries and Correspondence.*

Mützenberg, Gabriel — *Genève 1830.*

Ponsonby, Sir John — *The Ponsonby Family.*

Poulter, Louisa Frances — *Biographical Memoir of the Hon. William Robert Spencer* (first and third editions, the British Library).

Quennell, Peter — *Byron: The Years of Fame.*

Rogers, Samuel — *Recollections of the Table-Talk of Samuel Rogers,* edited by Morchard Bishop.

Rowse, A. L. — *The Later Churchills.*

Scott, Walter — *The Journal of Sir Walter Scott,* edited by W. E. K. Anderson.

Sichel, Walter — *The Glenbervie Journals.*

Smith, Horatio and James — *Rejected Addresses.*

Smith, Sydney — *Letters of Sydney Smith,* edited by Nowell C. Smith.

Spencer, F. Baron Churchill of Whichwood — *Lettre aux Genevois, 1821, Brochures genevoises, 1820-1830* (Archives de Genève).

Spencer, William Robert — 'Wife, Children and Friends', a ballad, from *English Songs and Ballads.*
Urania or the Illuminé, a comedy in two Acts (1802). Music by John Spencer.
'Leonore'. Translated from the German of Gottfried Bürger. Eds, 1798, 1808, 1809. Illustrations in the earlier edition by Lady Diana Beauclerk.
Poems (Collection 1811).
'Gelert's Grave or Llewellyn's Rashness. To which is added that Favorite Welsh Air, "Beddgelert", as sung by the Ancient Britons'.
Poems by the late Hon. William Spencer. A new edition with additions and a biographical memoir. 1835.
Carol: 'Listen to the Village Chime'. 1810. Music by John Spencer. (All the above in the British Library).
Sketch of the Character of the late Duke of Devonshire, with R. Adair, M.P. 1811. (Panshanger Papers).

Strickland, Margot — *The Byron Women.*

Van Muyden, B. — *Pages d'Histoire lausannoise.*

Wilson, Harriette — *Memoirs.*

Wraxall, Sir Nathaniel — *Historical Memoirs of my own Time.*

Ziegler, Philip — *Melbourne.*

PERIODICALS, NEWSPAPERS, ETC.

The Times.
The Morning Post.
Annual Register.
The Gentleman's Magazine.
The Weekly Register.
The Age.
The Satirist or Monthly Meteor.

The Satirist or The Censor of the Times.
The Miniature Magazine: or Epitome of the Times.
The Green Man or Periodical Expositor.
The Black Dwarf.
The English Annual for 1834.
Fisher's Drawing Room Scrap Book, 1832.
Journal de Genève, 1832, 1833, 1834.
Le Fédéral, 1835, 1836.
L'Europe centrale, 1834.
Revue du Vieux Genève, 1975
Almanach du Vieux Genève, 1948, 1960.

DIRECTORIES, GUIDES, ENCYCLOPAEDIAS, ETC.

The Complete Peerage.
Burke's Peerage.
Burke's Dormant and Extinct Peerages.
The Peerage and Baronetage of the British Empire, E. Lodge.
The Titled Nobility of Europe.
Dictionary of National Biography.
Répertoire des noms de familles suisses, 2nd ed.
Grand Larousse encyclopédique.
An Encyclopaedia of World History: Roumania, 1774-1916.
Cambridge Medieval History : The Byzantian Empire.
Oxford Companion to English Literature.
Cussans' History of Hertfordshire, Vol. IV.
Handbook of the Environs of London, James Thorne.
Lysons Environs of London, Vol. III.
Victoria County History (Essex, Surrey).
Grove's Dictionary of Music and Musicians.
Bryan's Dictionary of Painters and Engravers, 1734-1808.

MANUSCRIPT SOURCES

PANSHANGER PAPERS — By kind permission of Hertfordshire Record Office
and of Lady Ravensdale.
Boxes 9, 13, 16, 17, 18, 28, 37, 40 containing:
Letters:
    Lady Caroline Lamb, William Lamb, Lord Bessborough, the
doctors, letters to Augustus Lamb from various people, domestic
accounts, Susan's letters to Augustus and later to Lord Melbourne.

Lady Cowper to her brother Frederick Lamb.
William Lamb to his brother Frederick Lamb.
Lord Melbourne to Lady Brandon.
Lady Brandon to Lord Melbourne.
Mrs Caroline Norton to Lord Melbourne.
Letters to Lord Fordwich from members of the Cowper family.
Lord Melbourne's manuscript 'Autobiography'.

DEVONSHIRE MSS CHATSWORTH SIXTH DUKE'S GROUP — By kind permission of the Duke of Devonshire and the Trustees of the Chatsworth Settlement.

MELBOURNE HALL. LAMB PAPERS — By kind permission of the Marquis of Lothian.

BRITISH LIBRARY. DEPARTMENT OF MANUSCRIPTS — *Broughton (Hobhouse) Papers,* Add. MSS. 36.547, 36.460, 36.461, 36.464, 36.465, 34.466, 36.469. *W. R. Spencer,* Add. MSS. 39.898, f.50.

UNIVERSITY OF READING LIBRARY — By kind permission of Messrs. Longman, *Thomas Moore's Papers.*

PUBLIC RECORD OFFICE — Various Wills. Foreign Office Papers. FO 610, 612.

ARCHIVES D'ETAT DE GENÈVE — Registre de permis de séjour pour étrangers: Da/23432, 7388, 8076.

ARCHIVES CANTONALES VAUDOISES —Etat-Civil, Prilly, 1837, No. 23. Pièces justificatives. Visa des passeports: K VII g 11, 12. Album et catalogue des étudiants: Bdd. 107, 109. Dg, 122/1.

ARCHIVES DE LA COMMUNE DE LAUSANNE — Permis d'établissement, 320.

LOUISA SPENCER CANNING'S manuscript notebooks, in the author's possession.

SUSAN'S own written sources, apart from her letters in the Panshanger MSS, are her Journal, which runs intermittently from 1832 to 1850; the memorandum on its end page which she wrote for her children in 1848; and a copy of a letter by her husband, which was to be read after his death. All these documents are in private hands.

INDEX

Adelaide, Queen 81
Alvanley, 2nd Lord: William Arden 116
Anne, Queen 103, 104
Appia, Pauline 69, 70
Arbuthnot, Harriet 26, 29, 101, 103, 132
Ashley, Lord, later 7th Earl of Shaftesbury: Ashley Cooper 132, 133, 134, 135
Austen, Jane 85, 113

Bank of England 120, 125
Bavaria, Elector Palatine of 12
Beauclerk, Lady Diana XI, 12, 14, 23
Beauclerk, Topham 14
Bell, Andrew 65
Berteau, Melle 67, 68
Bessborough, 3rd Earl of: Frederick Ponsonby XII, 2, 3, 7, 38, 40, 50, 61, 80, 88, 89, 101, 113, 120, 135
Bessborough, Countess of: Henrietta Ponsonby XI, 2, 3, 6, 7, 8, 9, 10, 23, 35, 37, 38, 39, 44, 59, 61, 90, 101, 112, 116, 118, 130, 136
de Bétens, Elizabeth 69, 70
Birmingham Political Union 115
Blandford, Marquis of: See Marlborough, 6th Duke of Blandford, Marchioness of: Jane Spencer-Churchill 107, 118
Blattner, The Rev. 90
Bouverie, Mary 23
Brandon, Lady: Elizabeth Crosbie XIII, 1, 3, 56, 57, 58, 62, 71, 72, 73, 74, 76, 77, 78, 79, 80, 81, 82, 83, 87, 88, 89, 91, 122, 124, 130
Brandon, Lord: The Rev. William Crosbie 71
Brantôme, Pierre 57
Breadalbane, 1st Marquis of: John Campbell 118
Brooke, Lord: George Guy Greville 80
Brougham and Vaux, Lord: Henry Brougham 106
Bürger, Gottfried 14
Butin 67
Butler, Josephine 38
Byron, 6th Lord: George Gordon 3, 10, 18, 19, 20, 37, 44, 51, 52, 65, 69, 72, 116, 117, 119, 135

Campbell, Sir John 105
Cantacuzenus, Prince Basile of Moldavia 85, 88, 89, 93
Cantacuzenus, Prince Jean of Moldavia 85, 86, 87, 89
Caroline, Princess of Wales, later Queen 25, 106
Cavendish, Lady Harriet, later Countess of Granville - "Hary-o" XII, 8, 18, 20
Cerjat, Charles Sigismond 37, 38, 39, 51, 119, 120, 125
Charlotte, Queen 13
Chester, Mr 50
Chinnery, Mrs 23
Chinnery, Caroline 22, 126
Chinnery, William 21, 24
Churchill, Lords Charles and John: See Spencer-Churchill
Churchill, Susan Harriet Elizabeth, later Madame Cuénod 1, 2, 3, 4, 9, 24, 27, 28, 30, 34, 35, 37, 39, 40, 44, 45, 46, 50, 51, 55, 56, 57, 58, 59, 60, 61, 62, 64, 65, 66, 68, 69, 70, 72, 74, 77, 78, 79, 80, 81, 83, 84, 85, 86, 87, 88, 89, 90, 91, 93, 94, 96, 98, 101, 102, 103, 109, 110, 112, 113, 114, 116, 117, 118, 119, 120, 122, 124, 125, 126, 127, 128, 130, 131, 133, 134, 135, 136
Churchill, Susanna 98, 109, 111, 112
Coleridge, Samuel Taylor 18
Constant, Benjamin 78
de Constant, Charles 78
Conyngham, Lady Elizabeth 118
Cooper, Charlotte Barbara Ashley 132, 133
Courtney, Eliza 59, 61
Coutts Bank 105
Cowper, Emily, Countess XIII, 15, 34, 44, 45, 46, 52, 119, 135
Cowper, Lady Emily 15, 133
Crabbe, George 18
Creevey, Thomas 106
Crofts, Thomas (Tom) 55
Crosbie, Lilly (called Rosa by Susan) XIII, 58, 71, 72, 73, 74, 76, 77, 78, 79, 81, 83, 88, 89, 122
Crosby, Mrs. 55
Crosby boy, the 40
Cuénod, Aimé Timothée 93, 94, 96, 98, 122, 125, 126, 127, 128, 130

Cuénod, Caroline 122
Cuénod, Louise 120
Cuénod, William 122, 126
Cuénod-Churchill Bank of Vevey 126
Cunliffe, The Hon Emma, formerly Emma Crewe 80
Curtat, The Rev. Antoine 89, 90

Darby, John Nelson XIII, 91, 127, 128
Denman, 1st Lord: Thomas Denman 105, 106, 107, 116, 117
Devéria 58
Devonshire, Duchess of: Georgiana Cavendish XII, 6, 7, 8, 9, 11, 20, 21, 23, 35, 60, 61, 116, 124
Devonshire, 5th Duke of: William Cavendish XII, 6, 7, 9, 20, 25, 35, 61, 93
Devonshire, 6th Duke of: William Spencer Cavendish XII, 1, 8, 23, 24, 27, 28, 29, 38, 52, 90, 98, 111
Dudley, 1st Earl of: John William Ward 25, 26, 80

Edgeworth, Maria 1, 28, 30, 132
Edward VII, King 93
Egremont, 3rd Earl of: George O'Brien Wyndham 10
Elliott, Sir William 105
Englefield, Sir Harry 21, 25, 26, 27, 35, 133, 136

Ferriere, Louis Henry 69
Ferrière, Melle 68, 69, 70, 74, 76, 78, 80, 83
Ferrière, Monsieur le Pasteur 69, 76, 78
Follett, Sir William 105
Foster, Lady Elizabeth, later Duchess of Devonshire XII, 9, 19, 20, 25, 93, 124
Fox, Charles James 7, 10, 13, 14, 19, 20, 21, 23

Gage, Henry 73, 74, 76, 77, 79, 83
Gage, 4th Viscount of Castle Ireland: Henry Hall Gage 73, 76
Galatin, Pauline 69, 70
Galloway, 8th Earl of: George Stewart 118
Garlies, Lord: Randolph Stewart 105
George III, King 13
George IV, King 10, 12, 13, 14, 118, 119

Georgiana, illegitimate daughter of 5th Duke of Marlborough 134
Gibbon, Edward 19, 84
Glenbervie, 1st Lord: Sylvester Douglas 22
Glenorchy, Lord: John Campbell 105
Glover, Matilda 134
Goddard, Dr B 40, 44, 50, 51, 60
Grammont, Duc de 8
Granville, 1st Earl: Granville Leveson Gower 8, 9, 10, 37, 38, 61
Green, V. H. H. 134
Gregory, Barnard 105
Grenier, Auguste 87
Greville , Charles 106
Grey, 2nd Earl: Charles Grey 1, 9, 35, 61, 124

Hagard 44, 50
Hamilton, Lady 102
Hartington, Marquis of: See Devonshire, 6th Duke of
Hesse-Darmstadt, Margrave of 12, 27
Hobhouse, Sir John Cam, later 1st Lord Broughton XIII, 19, 25, 52, 72, 103, 115, 135
Holland, Lady: Elizabeth Fox 91
Hope, Thomas 21, 26
Hunter, Mrs 68

Jeans, Thomas 73, 74, 76, 79, 83, 84, 122
Jeffrey, Francis 113
Jenison Walworth, Dowager Countess 13
Jenison Walworth, Count Francis XI, 12, 14
Jenison Walworth, Countess Mary 32
Johnson, Dr. Samuel 14

Keate, John 114

Lacroix, Mr 79
Lafitte Bank 78
Lamb, Augustus XIII, 39, 40, 44, 45, 46, 50, 51, 56, 59, 94
Lamb, Lady Caroline XII, 1, 2, 3, 8, 10, 26, 37, 38, 39, 40, 44, 45, 46, 50, 51, 52, 55, 56, 57, 58, 59, 60, 61, 74, 80, 82, 90, 91, 101, 112, 116, 117, 118, 119, 130, 131, 133, 135, 136
Lamb, Charles 21
Lamb, Frederick, later 1st Lord Beauvale 34, 52
Lamb, George 10, 93

Lamb, William: See Melbourne, 2nd Viscount

Lancaster, Joseph 65

de Langalerie, Monsieur 91

La Touche, David 71

La Touche, Francis 79, 80

La Touche, Peter 79

Law, Susanna Adelaide XIII, 98, 101, 104, 105, 106, 107, 108, 109, 110, 111, 112, 113, 114, 116, 117, 118, 135

Lawson, Captain and Mrs: See Marlborough, 6th Duke of, and Miss Law

Lee, Dr Robert 51

Lees, Mr & Mrs 88

Leveson Gower: See Granville, Earl

Lieven, Princess 15, 25

Liszt, Franz 65

Lockhart, J. G. 6, 31

Louis XVI, King 6, 11

Lytton, Edward Bulwer, Ater 1st Lord Lytton 44

Mange, Melle 83, 84, 86, 87, 88, 89, 90, 120

Marie-Antoinette, Queen 6, 11, 12

Marlborough, 1st Duke of: John Churchill 29, 103, 116

Marlborough, 3rd Duke of: Charles Spencer 11, 14

Marlborough, 4th Duke of, George Spencer 101, 133

Marlborough, 5th Duke of: George Spencer-Churchill XIII, 1, 2, 101, 103, 110, 117, 132, 133, 134, 135, 136

Marlborough, 6th Duke of, Marquis of Blandford 1817-1840: George Spencer-Churchill XIII, 2, 27, 101, 102, 103, 104, 105, 106, 107, 108, 109, 110, 111, 112, 113, 114, 115, 116, 117, 118, 119, 132, 133, 134, 136

Marlborough, Duchess of: Susan Spencer-Churchill 105, 108, 110, 118, 136

de Mauley, 1st Lord: See Ponsonby, William Francis Spencer

Melbourne, Viscountess: Elizabeth Lamb XIII, 10

Melbourne, 1st Viscount: Peniston Lamb 40

Melbourne, 2nd Viscount: William Lamb XIII, 1, 2, 3, 4, 10, 14, 34, 37, 39, 40, 44, 45, 46, 51, 52, 55, 56, 57, 58, 59, 60, 61, 62, 69, 71, 72, 73, 76, 78, 81, 82, 83, 87, 88, 89, 90, 91, 93, 94, 96, 98, 101, 102, 105, 109, 110, 112, 113, 114, 118, 119, 120, 122, 124, 125, 126, 128, 130, 131, 133, 134, 135, 136

Mérienne, Melle 81, 82, 89

Mirabouc 67, 68

Monk, Miss 57

Moore, Thomas 13, 19, 21, 113

Mortimer, Miss 44

Murray, John 3, 18, 57

Murray, Lindley 57

Napoleon, Emperor 12, 13, 64, 65, 66

Napoleon de Paris 44

Necker, Jacques 11, 12

Neeld, Lady Caroline 80

Nelson of the Nile, 1st Viscount: Horatio Nelson 102, 118

Nelson, Horatia 102, 118

Norton, Caroline XIII, 3, 56, 59, 60, 61, 62, 71, 94

Norton, George 105, 124

d'Orléans, Charles 15

Ossulston, Lord: Charles Augustus Bennet 8

Ouiseau J. 57

de Palézieux Falconnet, Pierre 120

Parr, Dr Samuel 11

Paylis, Dr 87

Peacock, Mr & Mrs 50

Peel, Robert 115

Peligrine 76

Perdonnet, Vincent 93

Peterson, Sarah Harriet 44, 58, 59, 133

Pitt, William 19

Ponsonby, Lady Barbara 80, 81, 88, 89

Ponsonby, Lady Caroline: See Lamb, Lady Caroline

Ponsonby, Lady Emily 88

Ponsonby, Frances (Fanny) 40, 80, 89

Ponsonby, William Francis Spencer, later Lord de Mauley XII, 80, 88, 89, 120

Porta, The Rev. Charles 84, 90

Porta, François 84

Poulter, Louisa 4, 6, 30, 31

Regina v. Gregory 105, 107, 115

Rendlesham, Lady: Ann Thellusson 80

Richardson, Fanny 44, 45

Roe, Dr G. H. 40

Roe, James 40

Rogers, Samuel 13
de Ros, Henry William Fitzgerald, later Lord de Ros 1, 26, 27, 101, 111, 116, 132
Russell, illegitimate son of the Duke of Bedford 39

St John, Mrs: See Brandon, Lady
St Jules, Caroline, later Mrs. George Lamb XII, 9, 59, 93
Salisbury, Marchioness of 116
Scott, Sir Walter 6, 15, 18, 31, 65
Sheridan, Richard Brinsley 7, 13
Smith, Mr 79, 80
Smith, Horatio and James 18
Smith, The Rev. Richard 90
Smith, The Rev. Sydney 1, 13
Snow, Miss 67, 68
Spencer, Lord Charles 11, 101
Spencer, Charlotte 9, 60
Spencer, Francis Almeric, later Lord Churchill of Whichwood 65, 66
Spencer, Frederick 25, 26
Spencer, The Rev. George Trevor XI, 30, 103, 119, 126, 135, 136
Spencer, Georgiana, Countess 6, 7
Spencer, Harriet Caroline - "Harrio" - later Countess von Westerholt XI, 1, 2, 8, 9, 24, 26, 27, 28, 29, 30, 34, 35, 37, 38, 90, 98, 101, 102, 103, 110, 111, 112, 113, 114, 116, 117, 118, 119, 124, 132, 133, 135, 136
Spencer, Henrietta, Mrs George Trevor Spencer, formerly Henrietta Hobhouse 135
Spencer, John 11, 14, 31, 56
Spencer, Louisa Georgiana, later Mrs Canning XI, 22, 26, 30, 126
Spencer, Lord Robert 14
Spencer, Susan, Mrs William Spencer, formerly Countess Spreti XI, 12, 13, 18, 24, 25, 26, 27, 28, 29, 30, 61, 80, 101, 114, 126, 133
Spencer, William 22
Spencer William Robert XI, 1, 2, 4, 5, 6, 8, 10, 11, 12, 13, 14, 15, 18, 19, 20, 21, 22, 23, 24, 25, 27, 30, 31, 35, 61, 66, 80, 101, 113, 114, 118, 133, 136
Spencer-Churchill, Lord Charles 103, 104, 108, 112, 117
Spencer-Churchill, George: See Marlborough, 5th & 6th Dukes of
Spencer-Churchill, Lord John 103, 109, 110, 111, 114

Spenser, Edmund 21
Spreti, Count 12, 13
de Staël, Madame 12, 20, 78
Sterkey, Melle 67, 68
Sterkey, The Rev. Alexander 82
Stewart, Harriet Arundel 59
Stewart, James 105, 117
Stewart, Lady Jane: See Blandford, Marchioness of
Sturt, Lady Mary Ann 134
Sunderland, Earl of: John Winston Spencer-Churchill 104, 107, 110
Swiss Banks, Union of 126
Sysonby, Frederic 39

Thomson, Mrs 44
Trevor, General & Mrs 71, 72

de Vallière, Louis 84
de Vallière, Madame 85, 86, 87, 89
Victoria, Queen 3, 34, 56, 57, 120, 122, 127
Vigée-Lebrun, Madame 22
Villon, François 15, 22
Viotti, Giovanni 22
de Vos, Monsieur 86

Wales, Prince of: See George IV
Walpole, Horace 14
Warwick, 10th Earl and Countess of: Henry Richard and Sarah Greville 80
Webster, Miss 44
Wedgwood, Josiah 14
Wellington, 1st Duke of: Arthur Wellesley 1, 26, 50, 103, 115
von Westerholt, Count (Father of Charles) 28, 29
von Westerholt, Count Charles XI, 28, 29, 118
von Westerholt, Countess Harriet: See Spencer, Harriet Caroline
Westwood, Mrs 50
Wheeler, Rosina 44
William IV, King 94, 120
Williams, Miss 89
Williams, Charlotte 9, 59, 60, 130
Wilson, Harriette 51, 111
Wombwell, [George] 27, 116
Wordsworth, William 18, 21
Würtemberg, Prince, later King of 12, 13
Würtemberg, Princess Charlotte Augusta, later Queen of (formerly Princess Royal of England) 12, 13